W9-CSD-399

ART, MIND, AND RELIGION

Proceedings
of the
1965 Oberlin Colloquium
in Philosophy

Edited
by
W. H. Capitan
and
D. D. Merrill

UNIVERSITY OF PITTSBURGH PRESS

LIBRARY
SEP 10 1968
UNIVERSITY OF THE PACIFIC
187587

Library of Congress Catalogue Card Number: 67-13924

PRINTED IN ENGLAND
by C. Tinling & Co. Ltd., Liverpool, London, and Prescot

PREFACE

The essays in this volume were presented at the sixth annual Oberlin Colloquium held on April 16-18, 1965, by the Oberlin College Department of Philosophy. The principal contributors were invited to present papers on topics of their own choice and, if they wished, to prepare rejoinders to their commentators for publication. The result was a Colloquium which dealt with a wide variety of topics, including some not often discussed by philosophers in the analytic tradition.

In the first essay, P. H. Nowell-Smith attacks J. L. Austin's attempt, in *How to Do Things with Words*, to destroy "the assumption of philosophers that the business of a 'statement' can only be to 'describe' some state of affairs, or to 'state some fact,' which it must do either truly or falsely." He does so by arguing that Austin's distinctions and arguments do not successfully undermine the constative/performative and true/false dichotomies; that Austin does not successfully distinguish illocutionary acts from locutionary and perlocutionary acts; and that there are independent grounds for rehabilitating statements.

In the second essay, George Nakhnikian considers four formulations of St. Anselm's ontological arguments for the existence of God. He concludes that each of the arguments, while formally valid, uses at least one false premiss, and that attempts to overcome these difficulties do not succeed.

In the first symposium, Hilary Putnam proposes that being in pain be identified with a functional state of the organism. While rejecting *a priori* arguments against the identification of pain states and brain states, he argues that the functional-state hypothesis is to be preferred to both the pain-state and behavior-disposition theories on empirical and methodical grounds. Aune asserts that the functional-state hypothesis is essentially a formal characterization of pain, which is not inconsistent with the brain-state theory and does not involve an empirical theoretical identification of the usual kind. In addition, he asserts that the brain-state hypothesis, like many theoretical identifications, involves a change of meaning. U. T. Place contends that Putnam confuses mental states with mental processes, and that a functional process theory is not incompatible with the psycho-physical identity theory. He also suggests that the functional state (process) theory is not an empirical hypothesis, but rather a philosophical elucidation of the concept of pain in terms of a machine model.

In the second symposium, Stanley Cavell discusses the subject matter of aesthetics in light of the questions of fraudulence and trust presented by modern art and music. He claims that the dangers of fraudulence and of trust are essential to the experience of art and that the answer to the question "What is art?" will in part be an answer explaining why we treat certain objects in ways normally reserved for persons. Margolis suggests that Cavell's problem be treated as one of "borderline cases," keeping it separate from problems of value. Construing modernism in terms of the genuine and the fraudulent only intensifies the problem by reserving 'work of art' as an honorific term and insisting that we recognize in the new work what is genuine or fraudulent. Beardsley objects that formulating the problem in terms of fraudulence and genuineness begs too many questions; and, after arguing that contemporary developments in art show these notions to be irrelevant to proper aesthetic concerns, he offers his own solution by defining art broadly enough to include problematic cases. Cavell replies to these objections by claiming that they mistake his main purpose; and he tries to clarify it and other points in his paper by giving careful attention to the issues of intention, seriousness, and sincerity, and arguing for their relevance in proper aesthetic concerns.

In the third symposium, Ninian Smart argues that the description and interpretation of mystical experience depends in part on evidence not given in the experience itself, and that it is always important to ask about the degree to which non-experiential data are incorporated into descriptions of mystical experience. Pike objects that there can be purely phenomenological descriptions of mystical experience that do not involve theological presuppositions. Schmidt objects that Smart fails to notice the importance of putting the claims of each mystic into the context of his own conceptual system, and that he neglects the possibility of self-justifying mystical experience. Smart replies by saying that Pike's example can be interpreted so as not to refute his thesis. He accepts some of Schmidt's comments, but he adds that he is concerned mainly with theologically ramified descriptions and that his contentions are not shown to be wrong by his not discussing self-justifying mystical experiences.

The contributors to this volume are from nine colleges and universities in this country and abroad: Mr. Nowell-Smith from the University of Kent, Mr. Nakhnikian from Wayne State University, Mr. Putnam and Mr. Cavell from Harvard University, Mr. Aune from the University of Massachusetts, Mr. Margolis from the University of Western Ontario, Mr. Beardsley from Swarthmore

College, Mr. Smart from the University of Birmingham, Mr. Pike from Cornell University, and Mr. Schmidt from the University of New Mexico. Mr. Place is on the staff of Hollymoor Hospital, Birmingham, England.

Only two of the essays have appeared elsewhere in print. Mr. Nakhnikian's paper has been included in his *An Introduction to Philosophy*, and we wish to thank Alfred A. Knopf, Inc., for permission to publish it here. Mr. Smart graciously consented to be on the program when a scheduled speaker had to withdraw a short time before the Colloquium, and for the occasion he read portions of a paper previously promised to *Religious Studies*. We wish to thank Professor H. D. Lewis, the editor of that journal, for permission to include his paper.

The members of the Oberlin College Department of Philosophy wish to thank all those who attended the Colloquium for their active participation. They also wish to thank Oberlin College for its continuing support of the Colloquium. Finally, the editors are grateful to the contributors and to the staff of the University of Pittsburgh Press for their co-operation in preparing this volume.

CONTENTS

ACTS AND LOCUTIONS

P. H. NOWELL-SMITH

I. Austin's technique

First an old problem: Do we start with concepts ready made and learn to apply them to things as we go along, or do we start by bumping up against things in the world and learn, as Locke puts it, to "sort" them under names by abstraction? Whatever may be said against the former view—and "Platonism" is still a dirty word in some quarters—the latter view cannot be right. For it supposes that we *first* put all the lions on one side of the fence and all the non-lions on the other and *then* set about discovering what it is that all the lions have got and all the non-lions haven't got. And this can't be right since, if we lacked even a rudimentary concept of lion, we should not know on which side of the fence to put any object at all, and our process of examination could never get started.

I do not propose to discuss this problem in general or with respect to the question how we learn our native language; the old dilemma has a special interest for anyone who is introducing new technical terms, as Austin does in *How to Do Things with Words,*[1] and for anyone who is struggling to understand these new terms. What I have to say here is not just by way of preamble; it has a bearing on what I have mainly to say, which is that Austin does not—and perhaps with his technique cannot—succeed in "playing Old Harry with two fetishes which I admit to an inclination to play Old Harry with, viz: (1) the true/false fetish and (2) the fact/value fetish."[2] First, then, for Austin's technique and the hen-and-egg problem it raises.

Austin *invents* the word 'illocution' and introduces it in the following way. Having sorted out what it is to perform a "locutionary act" (to say something in the full normal sense of 'say') he writes:

> To determine what illocutionary act is so performed we must determine in what way we are using the locution:
> asking or answering a question
> giving some information or an assurance or a warning
> announcing a verdict or an intention . . .
> and the numerous like.[3]

[1] J. L. Austin, *How to Do Things with Words,* Oxford, 1962.
[2] *Ibid.,* p. 150.   [3] *Ibid.,* p. 98.

Now this is just a list of things that—in a very wide sense—we "do," and typically do with words. But how do we know what items to put into the list in the absence of any explicit criterion? Well, one obvious point about all the items in the list is that they are all things that we could be said to be doing "*in saying* something." This, then, is to be our test for what is an illocutionary act. But we now find that this test would let in such utterances as 'In saying *x*, I was mistaken, I was breaking by-law 22, I was forgetting that whales also are mammals, I was pretending to be The President.' Since this is a very heterogeneous bag, we shall, to be sure, have to recognize many sub-species, but they will all be, by definition, sub-species of the genus illocutionary act. Why not? It's his word, isn't it? (One obvious answer is that forgetting and being mistaken are not, in any serious sense, *acts* at all; but this answer won't do—or won't do just yet—because it is obvious that Austin is using 'act' and 'perform an act' in such a wide way that anything referred to by a verb capable of taking the name of a person as subject counts as an act; and for the moment at least we must allow him to do this.)

The reason why we reject these spurious items as members of the illocutionary club is simply that our intuitive noses tell us that they are beyond the pale. So now, having drawn up intuitively based lists of members and non-members, what we need is an articulate, explicit criterion for making the distinction. But, unless we are very lucky at the start, it is bound to happen that, whatever explicit test we come up with, we shall find that some of the items that our intuitive noses told us to admit will have to be rejected and *vice versa*. Thus we proceed dialectically, turning back and forth between intuitive list and explicit test until we reach one of two conclusions: either there never was any such animal as the illocutionary act and the whole enterprise has ended in failure, or we find that the revelations of our by now refined intuitive noses coincide exactly with the application of the explicit test. Now the point I want to make is this: at no point in this dialectical process would we have any reason for preferring our noses to the test or *vice versa* unless we were proceeding *throughout* on the assumption that illocutionary acts are *not* an arbitrarily constructed class, that there *is*, already *there*, a distinction that we are trying to track down. This assumption may, of course, be false; but unless we make it, the whole procedure is not merely pointless; it cannot be carried on at all.

The tests which Austin uses, both for making his distinctions—for example that between "illocutionary" and "perlocutionary"—and for constructing his lists, are all *verbal* tests such as: (1) Do we say "*In* saying *x* . . . " or "*By* saying *x* . . . " here? and (2) We can use *this* verb ('warn,' 'argue') in the first person present indicative, but not *that* verb ('alert,' 'convince'). But all this will give us is a list of verbs classified on the basis of which can and which cannot be used with such and such a construction; and this would be of no interest to anyone but a verbal botanist. The application of such tests will not help us to *characterize* what falls on either side of the lines; it will only enable us to draw the lines firmly. The difference between arguing and convincing is not just that there are grammatical differences between the verbs 'argue' and 'convince'; there are these grammatical differences between the verbs because arguing and convincing are different sorts of acts, *really* different. This is an assumption of Austinian method without which the enterprise would be trivial; and if this assumption is correct, it should be possible, not only to provide grammatical tests for the various classes of acts, but to characterize each class discursively. Austin sees this and goes some way toward meeting the demand when he tells us that acts are locutionary or perlocutionary by intention or by fact, but illocutionary by convention, and when he compares the sub-species of illocutionary acts with each other in the last lecture.

Austin's main aim in this book is to destroy "the assumption of philosophers that the business of a 'statement' can only be to 'describe' some state of affairs, or to 'state some fact,' which it must do either truly or falsely."[4] In Lecture XI the whole weight of the artillery he has been assembling is brought to bear on the target; and there are, I think, three ways in which the attack can be met. (1) We could sustain the barrage, relying on the impregnability of our Maginot Line. To drop the metaphor, we could give Austin his apparatus and all the conclusions he has reached so far and then try to show that his grand conclusion does not follow. (2) We could spike his guns, dismantle his missiles before they get off the ground, by showing that he has not made out all the distinctions he has claimed to make out and thus established nothing from which his grand conclusion could follow. (3) We could offer some independent arguments for rehabilitating statements.

II. Repelling the assault

Austin's main reasons for refusing to accord to statements their traditional primacy over other speech acts and even to admit that there is a general class of "statements" in the philosopher's sense are:

(1) The Constative Utterance cannot, as we used to think, be distinguished from the Performative Utterance, and
(2) Not all statements are true or false.

[4] *Ibid.*, p. 1.

Let us take each of these arguments in turn.

(1) The reasons originally given for distinguishing between constative and performative utterances were (a) that in a performative utterance we are not merely saying something, but also doing something; and (b) that performative utterances are liable to certain types of infelicity. But we are now in a position to see, says Austin, that "to state is every bit as much to perform an illocutionary act as, to warn or to pronounce,"[5] and "Once we realize that what we have to study is *not* the sentence but the issuing of an utterance in a speech situation, there can hardly be any longer a possibility of not seeing that stating is performing an act."[6]

Now the traditional philosopher can cheerfully agree that stating is, if not exactly "performing an act" (and one can imagine Austin being very severe about *that* phrase), at least *doing something* (namely stating). But Austin's dichotomy ("studying *not* the sentence *but* the issuing of an utterance") leaves out a possibly fruitful object of study—namely *what is said*. It is a surprising fact that Austin never seriously addresses himself to the familiar distinction between an "utter*ance*" (what is said) and an "utter*ing*" which he sometimes calls "the issuing of an utterance" (the saying of it). Words such as 'utterance,' 'statement,' 'judgment,' and 'warning' all have, in English, this ambiguity; and the attempt to translate Austin into Latin—where we have the distinction between 'judicatio' and 'judicatum'—would, I think, reveal a fundamental confusion. But this point, like the point that Austin never seriously addresses himself to the question "What is an *act*?" really belongs to the program of dismantling the missiles. For the moment I want to give Austin his concepts of "illocutionary act" and of "infelicity" and see whether he can use them to good effect. So let us turn to (1a).

(1a) *Is stating performing an illocutionary act, one among many such acts?*
Austin uses three arguments to show that stating is one among many illocutionary acts and "on a level with" the others.

   (i) We can say "In saying that it was raining, I was not betting or arguing or warning; I was simply stating a fact."[7]
   (ii) We can prefix to any statement, the formula 'I state.' Austin says that this shows 'I state' to be exactly on a level with 'I argue, suggest, bet,' etc.[8]
   (iii) As in the case of other illocutionary acts, it is essential to "secure uptake" and statements "take effect," e.g., in committing me to further statements.[9]

[5] *Ibid.*, p. 133.
[6] *Ibid.*, p. 138.
[7] *Ibid.*, p. 133.
[8] *Ibid.*, p. 133.
[9] *Ibid.*, p. 138.

None of these points seem to me to establish Austin's contention that stating is on a level with other illocutionary acts. For (i) though we can, as Austin says, say "In saying that it was raining I was not arguing; I was simply stating it was a fact," we *cannot* say "In saying that it was raining I was not stating that it was raining; I was simply arguing that it was." And it is the same with Austin's other example here:

> "In saying that it was leading to unemployment, I was not warning or protesting: I was simply stating the facts."

For here again, we could not say "In saying that it was leading to unemployment I was simply protesting: I was not stating that it was leading to unemployment." Of course one can protest against a policy on the grounds that it is leading to unemployment without *saying* anything; one could throw tomatoes; but one cannot protest *in this particular way*, namely by saying "it is leading to unemployment," without thereby stating that it is leading to unemployment. This is enough to show that, even if stating is an illocutionary act, it is not on a level with arguing, betting, protesting, etc. Some illocutionary acts involve stating, while others do not. One can suggest or guess that *p* without stating; but one cannot argue that *p* without stating it.[10]

(ii) Consider now the fact that it is possible to prefix 'I state/argue/suggest/bet' to the utterance 'He did not do it' as a way of showing that stating is one illocutionary act among many. This will not do; for (a) as before, some of these illocutionary acts involve stating while others do not; and (b) 'I state' differs from some of the others in this way also. If someone says simply "I argue that *p*," one might reply: "Well, go on, argue it; you haven't produced an argument yet." But if he says "I state that *p*," this reply cannot be made, since he has stated it.

(iii) Is stating like warning in that (a) it is necessary to secure uptake and (b) it takes effect, for example committing me to further statements? Austin's point about securing uptake seems to me in any case insecure; but if it is valid at all it would come in at the locutionary state. Have I successfully performed a locutionary act (said something in the full normal sense of 'say') in a communication situation if I have spoken *sotto voce* or so muffed the act that what I am saying is unclear? As to the point that statements "take effect," this seems to be another place at which Austin's

---

[10] Let no one say: "Of course you can; you can leave the conclusion of your argument unstated." For we are dealing, not with a psychological point about what you must say or may leave unsaid in order to get your point home to a particular audience, but with a logical point about the relations between arguments and conclusions.

failure to distinguish the uttering from the utterance is crucial. For, though the nature and extent of my commitments will no doubt depend on *what I have said*, it is *my saying of it* that commits me in the first place. "Taking effect" is a casual notion and therefore belongs to the uttering, not to the utterance.

(1b) *Are statements liable to infelicities?* Austin's second reason for abandoning the Constative/Performative distinction was that statements are liable to the infelicities he classified and named in Lecture II. But a careful examination of these will show, I think, that, with one possible exception to which I shall come in a moment, all these infelicities infect, not the utterance, but the uttering—or even some non-verbal feature of the performance, such as that it was the purser and not the captain who officiated or that the judge was not on the bench at the time. It may be impossible, in the case of the examples which Austin discusses in Lecture II, when he is still engaged on The Hunting of the Performative, to distinguish what is said from the saying of it; so let us look at what he now[11] says about the ways in which statements can be infelicitous. He makes three points here.

(i) Statements, like promises, can be insincere—as when I state that the cat is on the mat without believing that it is. There is a genuine parallel here, and I do not, of course, wish to *deny* that stating, like promising, is "doing something" and hence liable to some or all the infelicities that any "act" is liable to; but the insincerity lies, not in what I say, but in my saying it (while not believing it).

(ii) The statement that the present King of France is bald is not exactly false, but it is in some way outrageous. The failure here is a failure of *reference*[12] and Austin likens this case to that of a contract which is void on the grounds that some object to which it purports to refer does not exist—as when I contract to sell you a house which has been burnt down. Again there is a genuine parallel here, and we cannot now attribute the infelicity to the stating rather than to what is stated. This is clear if we take an example which avoids the complication introduced by the egocentric particular "present." 'Chimaeras are bald' is outrageous in just the same way, and here it is obvious that the infelicity lies in what it stated, not in the stating by someone at some particular time. Austin dismisses, without argument, the Strawsonian way out of saying that "the question does not arise" and he does not mention the Russellian way out

---

[11] *Ibid.*, p. 135-137.

[12] And should not this fact make Austin say that this is a *locutionary*, not an illocutionary failure? For the speaker has not used words "with a certain more-or-less definite sense and reference"; so he has not brought off a successful locutionary act.

according to which the statement is just false; so it is not clear what he would have said here. But if we give him his analogy with the void contract, we can see that there is also a difference. In the case of the void contract, though the *ground* of the infelicity, that which makes the contract infelicitous, lies in *what is contracted*, it is still the contract*ing*, the performance, which is infelicitous; but this is not true in the case of the outrageous statement.

(iii) Austin goes on to say: "Just as we often say 'You cannot order me,' in the sense 'You have not the right to order me,' which is equivalent to saying that you are not in the appropriate position to do so: so often there are things you cannot state—have no right to state—are not in a position to state. You *cannot* now state how many people there are in the next room . . . ."[13] But the trouble is that you *can* state this, even if you have no right to, are not in a position to state it. No matter what words he utters or what tone of voice he assumes nothing that the private says to the sergeant counts as an order. But if the policeman asks me for a statement about the rumpus that took place in the bar last night and, in spite of the fact that I was not well placed for seeing what went on, I give him a detailed account, what I say will certainly be called "my statement." Witnesses constantly make statements that they are not in a position to make, and thereby get tripped up by counsel; and this argument does not trade on any, possibly suspect, "philosophical" concept of statement. Statements made to investigating policemen and in the witness box are paradigm cases of statements in the plain man's sense.

To conclude this part of my argument, Austin may have convinced us that, in some quite general and unspecified sense of 'do,' stating something is just as much "doing something" as are promising, naming, and bequeathing—the paradigm cases of the old performative—and as are warning, arguing, protesting, and other paradigm cases of the new illocutionary act; and since stating is also doing, it is liable to some, at least, of the diseases which all doings are liable to. But we hardly needed convincing of this. What Austin has not shown is that stating is an illocutionary act, on a level with the others. I shall argue later[14] that stating is on a level with asking and telling and that these are not illocutionary acts, but forms of speech that can, each of them, have many illocutionary forces.

(2) Austin virtually concedes much of this when, having shown that constatives can be infelicitous, he writes: "Let us agree that all these circumstances of situation have to be in order for me to have succeeded in stating something, yet when I have, *the* question

[13] *Ibid.*, p. 137.
[14] p. 26-27 below.

arises, was what I stated true or false? And this, we feel, speaking in popular terms, is now the question of whether the statement 'corresponds with the facts.' With this I agree . . . So we have here a new dimension of criticism of the accomplished statement."[15] But he regards the concession as of little moment since he is going on to dissolve the true/false dichotomy itself. Here he uses two arguments. (a) There is a slide between true/false and other adjectives of assessment, since some illocutionary utterances, other than statements, can be true or false, or nearly so, and (b) some genuine statements are not true or false, or not exactly.

(2a) *Are illocutionary utterances, other than statements, true or false?* Austin produces two types of cases where there is "an obvious slide towards truth or falsity."[16] These are (i) verdictives such as estimating, finding, and pronouncing, and (ii) arguing soundly, advising well, judging fairly, and blaming justifiably.

(i) Of the verdictives Austin says that, though we should call estimates right or wrong and findings correct or incorrect and neither true nor false, "we shall certainly address ourselves to the same question," (namely "Does it correspond with the facts?"). I shall not challenge Austin's sensitive ear for English here; on this sort of point he is usually right; but the important question, as always, is "what philosophical conclusions can be drawn from these linguistic facts?" So, granting that we would not call estimates and findings true or false and that there is a reason for this,[17] what does this show? It does not seem to me to show that there is a *slide* between the true/false dimension and other dimensions, but rather that, whatever differences of nuance there may be, there is in one respect an *identity*. I estimate the distance from here to the tower to be 100 feet, and I have estimated rightly if the distance *is* 100 feet; the jury find the prisoner guilty, and their verdict is correct if the prisoner *is* guilty. The "correspondence with fact" claim in these cases seems to me to be the same claim as in the case of statements, not a rather similar claim. Estimates are not verdictives at all— pretension to finality being just what they lack—and genuine verdictives, such as those of the umpire or the jury, are, I shall argue later, statements which have a special illocutionary force in addition to being assessable in the true/false dimension.

(ii) Of the other group Austin asks: "Can we be sure that stating truly is a different class of assessment from arguing soundly, advising well, judging fairly and blaming justifiably? Do these not have

---

[15] *Ibid.*, p. 139.

[16] *Ibid.*, p. 140.

[17] Austin does not tell us what the reason is or even what different things are expressed by these different words; and he cannot really make his point about the "slide" without doing so.

something to do in complicated ways with facts?"[18] But I cannot see what force these rhetorical questions have as arguments. The answer to the second is "Of course they do!" A piece of advice or of blame will "have to do with facts" in this way, that one of the ways in which it can be infelicitous is that it presupposes a certain truth of fact. You cannot advise someone to apply for a job with total felicity if there is no such job; nor can you felicitously blame someone if he did not do whatever it was you are blaming him for. But from the true premiss that these activities have something to do in complicated ways with facts, you cannot derive the conclusion that Austin wants, namely that these activities are *like* stating truly. I see no reason for abandoning the traditional practice of telling students in their first logic lecture that statements can be true or false, arguments can be valid or invalid, and that these assessments, while being independent of each other, consummate a perfect marriage to bring forth an offspring in the form of a proved conclusion.

(2b) *Are some statements not (or not exactly) true or false?* Austin produces three examples of statements of which he thinks it will be difficult to say that they are true or false. In the order in which I shall take them these are:

    (i) All snow geese migrate to Labrador.
    (ii) Lord Raglan won the battle of Alma.
    (iii) France is hexagonal.

    (i) "Let us consider the question," writes Austin, "whether it is true that all snow geese migrate to Labrador, given that perhaps one maimed one sometimes fails when migrating to get quite the whole way?"[19] The difficulty is, as he says, that we do not understand the *reference* of such statements. But he has failed to notice that it is just *because* this is so that, if we hesitate to pronounce the statement true or false, this hesitation has no tendency to undermine the concept of the statement or the traditional way of identifying it as that which can be true or false. For, as long as we are unsure what the reference is, we cannot tell just *what statement it is* that we are being asked to pronounce true or false. Is the statement supposed to be that *all* snow geese migrate in the familiar logician's sense in which this is the contradictory of 'Some snow geese do not migrate'? If so, then, given that one maimed specimen fails to arrive, the statement is false. But of course, the catch lies in the fact that, in practice, no one would use this sentence to make *this* statement. Nor, I

---

[18] *Ibid.*, p. 141.
[19] *Ibid.*, p. 143. At this point I shall not comment in detail on the swans who come swanning in, because they only muddy the trail. Austin's point that reference depends on knowledge at the time seems both dubious and irrelevant.

think, would a circumspect ornithologist use this *sentence* to make *any* statement. He is far more likely to say "*The snow goose* migrates to Labrador," which, for all I know, is true, and which is certainly not refuted by the fact that some maimed specimens fail to get the whole way. This form of sentence 'The insect has six legs' is very common in natural history, and I would go so far as to maintain that 'Man has thirty-two teeth' could still be true even if no men ever had or will have thirty-two teeth.

(ii) The Lord Raglan case[20] suffers from ambiguity, not of reference, but of sense. The reason why we cannot pronounce it unhesitatingly true or false is not, as Austin thinks, that *it* can be judged true in a school text but not in a work of scholarship; it is that, if we take this *sentence* out of context, there is no "it" to be pronounced true or false. There is a convention governing the writing of school texts under which sentences of the form '*X* won the battle of *Y*' are used to make statements a sufficient condition of the truth of which is that *X* was the commanding general of the victorious side in the battle of *Y*. And if *this* is the statement being made, it is true; for it was Lord Raglan, and not for example Lord Cardigan, who was in command. But in works of scholarship there is a different and looser convention under which it is a necessary condition that the general must have played a decisive or at least a major role in the victory. In this sense "Napoleon won the battle of Austerlitz" is true, but "Lord Raglan won the battle of Alma" is false.

(iii) Of 'France is hexagonal' Austin writes that it is "good enough for a top-ranking general perhaps, but not for a geographer" and that it is "a rough description, not a true or false one."[21] I have left this example to the last because it is an example of fiendish ingenuity, its fiendishness consisting in this:

(a) "France is hexagonal" is, we want to say, certainly a statement.
(b) Austin has just come out in favor of the correspondence theory of truth.
(c) Matching a map to the ground is a paradigm case of "correspondence."

So, if we hesitate to say flatly that "France is hexagonal" is true or false, the game is up; we cannot defend the notion of the statement as that which is true or false if we hesitate to apply the true/false dimension of assessment to what is obviously a statement—and hesitate we certainly do. And we cannot deal with this example, as we did in the case of Lord Raglan, and say that the same sentence is used to make different statements in different contexts, some being

[20] *Ibid.*, p. 142.
[21] *Ibid.*, p. 142.

true and others false. For the doubt might easily arise within one context. Two top-ranking generals might dispute as to whether this description of France was or was not good enough (or true enough) for the purpose on hand. How rough are we allowed to get? We can only apply the true/false dimension of assessment if we are allowed to say that truth can be a matter of *degree*. So the philosophical questions that now face us are: (1) If we want to save the statement, defined as that which can be true or false, are we committed to a correspondence theory of truth and (2) if so, is it fatal to admit that truth can be a matter of degree? I shall not attempt to answer these questions, saying only (1) that the weakest form of correspondence theory ('*p*' is equivalent to *p* is true), while a useful device for kicking semantics out of logic, is of no help here; (2) that stronger forms of correspondence theory (one-to-one correspondence, picture theory and the like) are highly suspect; and (3) that if Austin really wants to play Old Harry with the true/false fetish, it is not sufficient to point out that, in the case of some predicates, truth and falsity may be a matter of degree. He must show this admission to be fatal.

One last general point about all the examples: Austin is supposed to be showing us that, in the case of some utterances that are undoubtedly statements, we hesitate to apply the true/false dimension of assessment; but what his examples would actually show (if they showed anything) would be that in some cases we hesitate between 'true' and 'false'; and these are not at all the same thing.

III. Dismantling the missiles

The second way in which I suggested that Austin's attack could be met was by showing that he has failed to make out satisfactorily all the distinctions of which his arsenal is composed. This could, I believe, be done all along the line, from the first distinction between phonetic, phatic, and rhetic acts; but this would take too long, and anyway this trio drops pretty soon below the horizon. So I shall concentrate on the key question whether Austin successfully distinguishes illocutionary acts from locutionary and perlocutionary ones.

The first test which Austin uses for distinguishing illocutionary from perlocutionary acts is the possibility of using the 'I'-form of the verb, and it is to this test that he returns when he compiles his classified list of illocutionary acts in Lecture XII. But, as I suggested in the first section, this test, being purely verbal, gives us no insight into the nature of the distinction. It was perhaps for this reason that Austin turned, in Lecture X, to another verbal test which, he tells us, will certainly *not* do, but which may give us more insight. It is in this Lecture that he tries to establish a point that he makes many times and clearly regarded as most important: that while locutionary and perlocutionary acts are constituted as such by intention or by fact, illocutionary acts are constituted as such by *convention*.[22] What can we make of this?

(1) *Are illocutionary acts conventional acts?* Is there anything specially *conventional* about an utterance's being illocutionary over and above the old Greek sense in which all expressions mean what they do mean by convention (*nomo*) and not by nature (*physei*)? It is by convention that a red flag means danger, and also by convention that 'red' means red, that 'warn' means warn, and that 'alert' means alert. One point is clear: perlocutionary verbs import a reference to *consequences* and the question whether or not a perlocutionary act (alerting or convincing someone) has been brought off will depend on what someone subsequently does—and this is a matter, not of convention, but of fact. But (a) this test will not distinguish the illocutionary from the locutionary, since the question whether or not I have brought off a locutionary act will be one of convention, the conventions governing the sense and reference of words, and (b) it does not show that illocutionary acts are conventional in some stronger sense than the old Greek one, and this must be Austin's intention.

One point that Austin makes here is that "A judge should be able to decide, by hearing what was said, what locutionary and illocutionary acts were performed, but not what perlocutionary acts were achieved."[23] But what does this show? (a) If "what was said" is allowed to include what someone else said *after* the act in question was performed, the judge could, in some cases, decide what perlocutionary act had been achieved. For example, if the evidence shows that the respondent said "O.K. I'll do it," the judge could decide that a perlocutionary act of persuading had been achieved. Austin must exclude from the evidence before the judge, not only what various people subsequently *did*, but also what they subsequently *said*, if he is to use the test of "hearing what was said" as a way of distinguishing the illocutionary from the perlocutionary. For what distinguishes the illocutionary from the perlocutionary here has nothing to do with the *conventionality* of the latter at all; it is the old point that, for a perlocutionary act to be successfully brought off, someone has *subsequently* to say or do something—or, significantly, nothing.[24]

---

[22] *Ibid.*, pp. 103, 105, 108, 118, 120, and 127. In the last of these passages Austin winds up with the words: "These features serve to pick out illocutionary acts most satisfactorily." It is a thousand pities that the text of the two preceding pages is so corrupt that we cannot determine what "these features" are.

[23] *Ibid.*, p. 121.

[24] 'By saying . . . I put him at his ease/sent him to sleep' is perlocutionary.

(b) If, on the other hand, we take Austin to mean that the judge hears literally nothing but *what was said*, with nothing in the evidence about the context, he will not, on Austin's own showing, be able to decide what locutionary act had been achieved. The question is whether there is anything specially conventional about what the judge must hear in order to decide what illocutionary acts were performed, and I don't think that Austin has shown that there is.

Let us look at this dialectically. Austin winds up with a classified list of illocutionary verbs constructed on the principle that every verb in the list passes the 'I'-form test, a verbal test. Can we, having got our list, proceed to detect anything specially *conventional* that all the acts corresponding to these verbs have in common? In many cases we can. What leaps to the eye is that some of these verbs are a survival from the old Hunting of the Performative. (To say "I bequeath" in suitable circumstances *is* to bequeath. To say "I promise" in suitable circumstances *is* to promise.) Others, again, have a strong smell of the law courts—for example 'acquit,' 'contract,' 'rule,' 'hold as a matter of law that . . .,' 'find as a matter of fact that . . . .' Now it is a special feature of all the paradigm cases of performatives[25] that they involve a special ceremonial, ritual, or procedure, and it is a special feature of courts of law—one might almost say that it is *the* special feature of courts of law—that they give a tightly regulated aspect to what might otherwise be pretty indefinite procedures. This is what makes the difference between giving a promise and *signing a contract*, between telling someone something in a casual way and *stating something on oath*, between avoiding someone and *excommunicating* him. The operations of the law are conventional in a sense over and above the trivial sense in which all language is conventional, in that they are governed by a complicated and articulate set of man-made rules: only the jury can convict or acquit, only the judge can sentence or hold as a matter of law, etc. It is "by convention" in the trivial sense that 'acquit' means acquit and also that 'lion' means lion. But acquittals, convictions, and the rest are themselves *conventional objects* in a sense in which lions are not.

But we cannot say the same about *all* the verbs in Austin's list. To pick at random one example from each of his five classes, what are the *conventions* governing 'I diagnose,' 'I urge you to . . . ,' 'I am determined to . . . ,' 'I deplore,' or 'I would describe it as . . . ' over and above the trivial fact that it is by convention that all these

[25] Except promising; but it is *just this absence* of a recognized ritual or procedure in the case of promising, combined with the fact that 'I promise' is so clearly performative, that gives rise to one of the philosophical problems about promises. How in the world did the mere fact of uttering the words 'I promise' come to have the special force that distinguishes a promise from a "mere" expression of intention or prediction? How did Hobbes's savages ever get together to sign the Original Contract?

words mean what they do mean? Why did Austin say that you cannot now state how many people there are in the next room? Because you are not in a position to do so. Certainly; but this is quite different from the way in which you, not being the umpire but only a spectator, cannot declare the batsman out. The spectator's not being in a position to declare is by convention, but your not being in a position to state how many people there are in the next room is constituted by fact.[26]

Austin has, I think, been misled here in a very subtle way. He has seen that there is something special and important about verbs which have the 'I'-form. He then slips into contemplating those cases in which we actually *do* (or *might*, in some stronger sense than mere grammatical possibility) use the 'I'-form, where, for example, we start our warning utterance with 'I warn you that . . . .' But he has failed to see that to concentrate on these is to concentrate on cases that have a *solemnity* which immediately transports us into a church, court of law, cricket field, or other convention-ridden environment.

(2) *Are illocutionary acts intentional acts?* Whether or not there is necessarily anything conventional about illocutionary acts, there is certainly something intentional about them. One can, of course, warn someone inadvertently, accidentally or by mistake. But when someone makes the illocutionary force of his utterance clear by prefixing 'I . . . ,' this must be intentional. For the original point of using the 'I'-form test for illocutions was that it was by means of this formula that we make it clear what illocutionary force our utterance has; and we cannot make clear what illocutionary force our utterance has without intending it to have that force. Acts of warning, promising, apologizing, and so on are constituted as the acts they are partly by its being the intention of the speaker to warn, promise, apologize, etc.

Can one promise or apologize without intending to do so? We must distinguish here two different cases. (a) There are cases where there is a discrepency between the "primary" and the "explicit" performance: I promise without intending to perform, apologize without really feeling sorry. These are insincerities, and they are not exceptions to the principle that illocutionary acts are intentional acts; for I *do intend* to promise or apologize. But (b) there might be cases where I utter the promissory or apologetic words (and *have* therefore promised/apologized) inadvertently, in a moment of abstraction, not thinking what I was saying, not really knowing

---

[26] I am not here trading on the spatial sense of 'being in a position to.' With the restrictions that Austin places on 'stating,' you are not in a position to state anything if you are not an expert or do not have special knowledge; and experts are (one hopes) experts by fact, not by convention.

what I was doing. These are genuine exceptions, but they do not refute the thesis that illocutionary acts are intentional acts, if that thesis is properly understood. For like most such theses in philosophy, it is not intended to be literally true of *all* cases; it is intended to characterize the standard or primary case, and these cases of inadvertency are necessarily parasitic, in the sense that we could not have the concepts of promising and apologizing inadvertently unless we had the concepts of promising and apologizing intentionally, i.e. with full knowledge of what we are doing. This, of course, would need to be argued, and one sketch of an argument would be: Could a child learn what it is to promise or to apologize in a world in which all promises and apologies were inadvertent?

(3) *Are there illocutionary and perlocutionary acts?* Austin, as I remarked near the beginning, gives no account of what it is to perform an (intentional) act. If I (a) say "It's about to charge" and in saying this (b) warn someone that the bull is about to charge and (c) alert him, Austin tells us that I have performed three acts, respectively the locutionary, the illocutionary, and the perlocutionary. He agrees, of course, that these three acts are "only abstractions" and that the only concrete reality here is the total speech act in its total social context; and we can agree with him that it might be useful to distinguish different aspects of this concrete reality. But what is the point of making these distinctions in terms of a number of different acts that I am said to perform? Austin's reason for so doing is that 'say,' 'warn,' and 'alert' are all *verbs*; but this is only a reason for distinguishing different acts if we assume that all verbs are names of acts. He seems to think that verbs "stand for" or "refer to" acts in the way that nouns "stand for" or "refer to" things. But that theory got us into notorious troubles by hypostatizing some pretty queer things, such as unpunctuality, the probability of my dying next year, etc., and in the same way Austin's theory hypostatizes some pretty queer acts. This is unfortunate since one of the ways of getting out of the old name-thing difficulties was to drop abstract nouns and concentrate on adjectives, adverbs, and verbs. (As Austin himself once remarked "*In vino*, possibly, '*veritas*'; but in a sober symposium '*verum*'.")[27]

If saying is really also doing in a serious sense of 'do,' the standard or primary cases which most deserve our attention must be those in which we say something (a) intentionally, i.e., knowing what we are saying and intending to say it, and (b) purposively, i.e., intending not just to say it but to bring about some effect or consequence; and it is for this reason that "In saying *p*, I was forgetting/mistaken" must be rejected as not genuinely illocutionary. But if this is right,

[27] J. L. Austin, *Philosophical Papers*, Oxford, 1961, p. 85.

Austin would have done better to couch his theory, not in terms of acts, but in terms of illocutionary *forces* and perlocutionary *objects*, as indeed he often does. What will then emerge is a theory in which the illocutionary forces turn out to be our intentions-in-saying-something and the perlocutionary objects will be our achieved purposes. Now Austin himself rejects this doctrine, but the arguments that he uses (for example that some perlocutionary effects are unintended) not only are, but *must be* insufficient. For if it is always open to us to reject 'In saying *p*, I was forgetting' as not genuinely illocutionary, why should we not be allowed to reject 'By saying *p*, I convinced him that I was a fool' as not genuinely perlocutionary? In the end, because the technical terms are of our own invention, we can decide how to use them, and the only reason for using them in one way rather than another is that one new theory may be enlightening and the other not.

IV. Rehabilitating the statement

Austin refers only once[28] to the possibility that an utterance might have two illocutionary forces at the same time, and this is in connection with a complicated example drawn from the game of bridge. From this it appears that he thought that a double illocution would be a rare specimen of more interest to a verbal botanist than to a serious philosopher. But in fact, if we look at his final list of illocutionary verbs, we find that double illocutions are as common as corn in the corn belt. When the foreman gives the jury's verdict, he *also* answers the judge's question "Do you find the prisoner guilty or not guilty?" and in general any answer to a question will always have some illocutionary force other than that of being an answer to a question; it will be a statement, verdict, estimate, request, and so on; and this suggests that 'answering' either belongs to the locutionary stage or that we should invent a new class of acts between the locutionary and the illocutionary. 'Asking' would also go into this class; for we could say "In asking the question 'what was the date of the battle of Hastings?' I was not seeking information but testing the candidate's knowledge!" Similarly 'telling someone to do something' is not really illocutionary. For it would be at best very odd to say "In saying 'Go away,' I was telling him to go away," but it would not be in the least odd to say "In telling him to go away, I was requesting/advising/ordering him to go away," or to say that my telling him to go away *had the force of* a request, piece of advice, or an order. 'Asking' and 'telling' thus seem to be like 'saying' in that they would occupy the X rather than the Y position in the formula 'In X-ing, I was doing Y.' (They are unlike 'saying' in that

[28] *Ibid.*, p. 129.

asking and telling are subsumed under saying in the locutionary sense of 'say.') I want now to suggest some reasons for elevating 'state' to the level of 'ask' and 'tell.'

Suppose that A and B each say "Jones is guilty" and thereby perform the same locutionary act in that by 'is guilty' they both mean is guilty, and that by 'Jones' they both refer to the same man. A is the foreman of the jury giving the verdict, and B is a spectator in the gallery giving his own opinion to anyone who cares to listen. There is a stronger sense of 'say' than the merely locutionary in which they have both said the same thing, viz: that Jones was guilty. For C, another spectator, might "say the same thing" in the locutionary sense but in a questioning tone of voice, and there is a sense in which he has not *said that* Jones was guilty at all; he was asking whether Jones was guilty. Now it is just here, to point to what both A and B did, but C did not do, that the philosopher wants to speak of A and B *stating* or *asserting* that Jones was guilty. Austin won't let him do this, on the grounds that 'state' and 'assert' have their own special meanings. But how much ice does this cut?

Austin never wanted to place a general ban on (a) the introduction of new words or (b) the use, in a wider sense, of a word that normally has a narrower sense, on some such grounds as that ordinary language must be in order as it is. What he would argue at this point would be that these practices are dangerous and that, if ordinary language lacks a word or a wide use of a word, we should make sure that there is a need to introduce the new word or the new usage. To do so without clear need is to draw a malodorous red herring across the trail. This may, in general, be good advice; but it won't do here. For ordinary language does, in this case, recognize the philosopher's "statement" and does have a word for it, though it is none of the philosopher's favorite words, 'state,' 'assert,' 'judge,' or 'propound.' It is, in one of its senses, the verb 'to say.' 'Say' can mean "utter noises belonging to a language with a certain more-or-less definite sense and reference," Austin's "locutionary" or "full normal" sense; but it can also be used to mean what the philosopher means by 'state' or 'assert.'[29] We need, and also have a general word for all those cases in which someone "comes right out and says something" (as opposed to merely hinting or suggesting or ruminating) and for those cases where we want to say that two people "said the same thing" but with different illocutionary forces.

Austin, I want to suggest, may have fallen into a trap into which many philosophers of law have fallen. For obvious reasons, cases

[29] Another place where we need the wide concept of "statement" is in logic, though logicians who don't mind saying one *sentence* can imply another may not feel the need; but let's not start this hare now.

which become *causes célèbres* and get widely discussed in the learned
journals are cases which have some interesting and unusual feature,
and theories as to "what the law really is" are often built on a
study of these cases, to the neglect of the far more common and
therefore less interesting cases. In much the same way Austin's
interest in, and uncommon fertility in the production of off-beat
examples may have blinded him to the standard cases right under
his nose. Do we not recognize the broad distinction between
stating, asking, and telling in the existence of the indicative,
interrogative, and imperative forms of speech? Yes, comes the
reply; but grammatical mood is an unsure guide. For orders can be
given in the future indicative mood, indeed are commonly so
given in the army; and we can sometimes wonder whether an
utterance in the indicative mood did not have the force of a question.
The reply to this is: Sometimes; but only *sometimes*, not *always*. It is
only when a remark is made in a grammatical form or in a tone of
voice that is *not* the standard form or tone for that sort of remark,
that we can say that what he said, though in the indicative mood,
was "really" a question or that, though he said it in the interrogative
mood, it was "really" not a question, but an order. ("Do you want
to shut the door?" can sometimes be an order.)

There are, to be sure, occasions on which there is something
special about the context which makes us suspect that a remark
which "looks like" a statement—ought, so to speak, to be a statement—is "really" a question or an order; and it is the fact that we
can raise such doubts that has led Austin to treat "saying," "asking,"
and "telling" as illocutionary forces that remarks can have. But,
if someone says, "The cat is on the mat," in absolutely standard
conditions, we *cannot* ask if his utterance has the force of a statement,
and if he says, "Is the cat on the mat?" in absolutely standard
conditions, we cannot ask whether he has asked a question. It is for
this reason that I am tempted to bring in the concepts of saying,
asking, and telling at the locutionary stage. If someone says, "The
cat is on the mat," in standard conditions, and I characterize his
utterance as one of using these words with sense and reference, but
do not further characterize it as stating something, have I really
characterized it as a "full unit of speech?"

ST. ANSELM'S FOUR ONTOLOGICAL ARGUMENTS*

GEORGE NAKHNIKIAN

No ontological argument for God's existence can be either conclusively refuted or conclusively established at present because every known, and presumably every conceivable, ontological argument for God's existence involves profoundly controversial and unsettled questions in logic. Is existence a property? Is the *PM* semantical interpretation of the existential quantifier adequate? What is a proper name? And if some ontological arguments should not involve these questions, there is another question that they are almost certain to involve, namely, the question: Should we countenance quantification in modal contexts? And even if those questions are answered to everyone's satisfaction, it would not follow that we would have a way of proving that it is in principle impossible to construct a cogent ontological argument for God's existence. We must, in short, still examine every proposed ontological argument on its individual merits.

Sometime ago Charles Hartshorne and more recently Norman Malcolm discerned two distinct ontological arguments in St. Anselm. In this paper I propose to examine not two but four Anselmian arguments. They are strongly suggested, if not explicitly found, in St. Anselm. The first three were given to me by William Rowe. The fourth formulation is attributed to R. M. Chisholm. W. C. Salmon and I discussed Chisholm's formulation in a joint paper sometime ago,[1] and here I want to jot down some further thoughts on it.

I. St. Anselm's first ontological argument

(1) It is possible that God exists.

(2) It is not possible that there exists a being greater than God.

(3) For any property ϕ, if nothing is ϕ although it is possible that something is ϕ, then it is possible that there exists something which is ϕ and there exists something which is greater than the thing which is ϕ.

∴ (4) God exists.

* —Copyright 1967 by George Nakhnikian. Reprinted with some revisions by permission of Alfred A. Knopf, Inc. from the author's *An Introduction to Philosophy*.
[1] See " 'Exists' as a Predicate," *Philosophical Review*, LXVI, 1957, pp. 535-542.

The second premiss is one way of saying that God is supremely perfect. The third premiss formulates the idea that an actually existing being is greater than one which is only possible. Because the English sentences may be ambiguous, let us formulate the argument unambiguously by rendering it in standard logical notation.

(1) $\Diamond$ ($\exists x$) Gx
(2) $\sim \Diamond$ ($\exists x$) [Gx . ($\exists y$) (y is greater than x)]
(3) (ϕ) ($\sim(\exists x)$ ϕx . $\Diamond$ ($\exists x$) ϕx) $\supset$ $\Diamond$ ($\exists x$) (ϕx . ($\exists y$) (y is greater than x))
∴(4) ($\exists x$) Gx

The argument is valid but not sound. Its third premiss is false. Let ϕ = being an entity equal in greatness to every other entity.[2] Now, it is true that:

(a) It is not the case that there is an entity equal in greatness to every other entity, although it is possible that there is an entity equal in greatness to every other entity.

But it is false that:

(β) It is possible that there exists an entity equal in greatness to every other entity while there exists an entity greater than it.

Thus, we have an instance of (3) with true antecedent and false consequent. Hence, (3) is false.

A way out of this difficulty may be to reject the general principle, (3), and to work with a premiss that is about God only. The argument now is as follows:

(1) $\Diamond$ ($\exists x$) Gx
(2) $\sim \Diamond$ ($\exists x$) (Gx . ($\exists y$) (y is greater than x))
(3) ($\sim(\exists x)$ Gx . $\Diamond$ ($\exists x$) Gx) $\supset$ $\Diamond$ ($\exists x$) (Gx . ($\exists x$) (y is greater than x))
∴(4) ($\exists x$) Gx

The argument is formally valid. But not all of the premisses are beyond doubt. I am prepared to grant that (1) and (2) are necessarily true. But as (2) is necessarily true, the consequent of (3) is necessarily false. Hence, if (3) is necessarily true, then its antecedent is necessarily false. But the antecedent of (3) is not necessarily false. Hence, (3) is not necessarily true. Hence, the argument does not prove that necessarily God exists. The only controversial claim I have made is that the antecedent of (3) is not necessarily false.

[2] This example was suggested by Hector-Neri Castañeda.

On the face of it, it seems perfectly consistent to think that although it is possible that God exists, in fact God does not exist. If the defender of the ontological argument believes otherwise, the burden is on him to prove that the belief in question which seems to be perfectly consistent is really necessarily false. The ontological argument which we are now examining proves no such thing.

There is one more move open to the defender of this ontological argument. He may admit that perhaps (3) is not necessarily true but insist that (3) is contingently true. Now, still assuming that the consequent of (3) is necessarily false, (3) is contingently true only if its antecedent is contingently false. But anyone who has admitted that it is possible that God exists and is thinking clearly will admit that the antecedent of (3) is false only if he admits that "God does not exist" is false. Now anyone who doubts that God exists will have no reason to change his mind about God's existence on the basis of anything he has been told so far. Hence, he will have been given no reason for believing that "God does not exist" is false. He will have been told dogmatically that (3) is true, but he will be under no rational compulsion to believe what he is told. Hence, although everyone would grant that if (1) and (2) are necessarily true and (3) is contingently true, then it is true that God exists, no one, not even those who believe that (3) is true, has any reason for insisting that the conclusion has been proved true. For, on the basis of anything said so far, no one has any reason for believing that (3) is true.

Let us try one more emendation. This time we shall make use of St. Anselm's distinction between *existing in the understanding* and *existing outside the understanding*. Let us read:

'$(\exists^1 x)$' as *in the understanding there exists an x such that* . . .
'$(\exists^0 x)$' as *outside the understanding there exists an x such that* . . .

The argument now reads as follows:

(1) $\Diamond \ (\exists^0 x) \ Gx$
(2) $\sim \Diamond \ (\exists^0 x) \ (Gx \ . \ (\exists^0 y) \ (y \text{ is greater than } x))$
(3) $\{(\exists^1 x) \ Gx \ . \ \sim (\exists^0 x) \ Gx \ . \ \Diamond \ (\exists^0 x) \ Gx\} \supset \Diamond \ (\exists^0 x)$
$(Gx \ . \ (\exists^0 y) \ (y \text{ is greater than } x))$
(4) $(\exists^1 x) \ Gx$
∴ (5) $(\exists^0 x) \ Gx$

Translated into English, the argument is as follows:

(1) It is possible that outside the understanding God exists.
(2) It is not possible that outside the understanding God exists and also that outside the understanding there exists a thing greater than God.

(3) If in the understanding there exists a thing which is God, and outside the understanding no God exists and it is possible that outside the understanding God exists, then it is possible that outside the understanding God exists and also that outside the understanding there exists a thing greater than God.

(4) In the understanding God exists.

∴(5) Outside the understanding God exists.

The argument is valid, but it suffers from exactly the same defect as the immediately preceding version. This time, granted that (1) and (2) are necessarily true, the consequent of (3) is necessarily false. Hence, if (3) is necessarily true, then its antecedent is necessarily false. But the antecendent of (3) is not necessarily false. Hence (3) is not necessarily true. The claim that the antecendent of (3) is not necessarily false seems to be obviously true. The present version of the ontological argument provides no reason whatever for thinking otherwise. Hence, the argument does not establish the truth of its conclusion. That this is so we know without having to decide what is meant by 'existing in the understanding' and 'existing outside the understanding.' All we need is the supposition that these expressions can be interpreted in such a way as to make every step of the argument a proposition, something that can be true or false.

Nothing will be gained by claiming that (3) is contingently true. We have already gone through the sort of argument that shows the futility of this last ploy.

II. St. Anselm's second ontological argument

(1) It is possible that there exists a being whose non-existence is impossible.

(2) If it is possible that x does not exist, and it is possible that there exists a being whose non-existence is impossible, then it is possible that there exists a being greater than x.

(3) It is not possible that there exists a being greater than God.

∴(4) It is not possible that God does not exist, or it is not possible that there exists a being whose non-existence is impossible. (By (2) and (3))

∴(5) It is not possible that God does not exist. (By (1) and (4))

The trouble with the argument is in the first two premises. By "a being whose non-existence is impossible" we are presumably to understand *a necessarily existing being*. But what sort of property is necessary existence? In ordinary contexts we use 'necessary' adjectivally in such examples as:

He has the necessary courage to face the danger.

He has the necessary intelligence to pass the test.

He has the necessary self-control to resist her sexual blandishments.

In these and relevantly similar cases the adjectival use of 'necessary' has the force of "sufficient," "enough of what it takes to" complete some task, realize a goal. Necessary courage and just plain courage are not two different properties. There is no such property as necessary courage. Similarly, even if *existence* were a property, there is no such property as *necessary existence*.[3] Hence, the first two premises of the second ontological argument are false. This is easy to see if we notice that 'x is P' is short for 'x has the property P.' But "x has the property P" entails that P is a property. Therefore, if P is not a property then every proposition of the form "x is P" is false. As necessary existence is not a property, "x necessarily exists," "it is possible that x necessarily exists," "it is necessary that x necessarily exists" are all false. Or, even worse, they are meaningless. 'He has the necessary courage' is a meaningful sentence because we know what 'necessary courage' means. But we really do not know what 'necessary existence' means if it is supposed that necessary existence is a property; hence the sentences 'God necessarily exists,' 'It is possible that God has necessary existence' and 'It is necessary that God have necessary existence' could be said to be unintelligible.

God has necessary existence could mean that it is necessarily true that God exists. Now premiss (1) would be saying the following:

(a) It is possible that it is necessary that something exists.

But "it is possible that it is necessary that something exists" entails "It is necessary that something exists." Hence, we cannot know (a) to be true unless we know that it is necessary that something exists. But we know that it is necessary that something exists. For instance, it is necessarily true that properties exist. The proposition:

Whatever is red is red

is logically true; hence, it is necessarily true, and it entails the proposition:

There is a property such that whatever has it is red.

This proposition itself is necessarily true because it is deducible from a necessarily true proposition. Hence, it is necessarily true that properties (e.g., the property of being red) exist. Thus, if (1) is identical with the proposition that it is possible that it is necessary that something exists, then (1) is true.

But (2) is implausible. It says in effect that a thing whose existence is necessary may be greater than anything which does not exist.

[3] Cf. Paul Henle, "Uses of the Ontological Argument," *Philosophical Review*, LXX, 1961, pp. 102-109.

c

Imagine a thing which has all the perfections of God but lacks existence. Is it obvious that the property of being red may be greater than it? Far from it. In fact, the following seems to be a plausible definition:

> x is more perfect than y = Df. x resembles a supremely perfect being more than y resembles it.

If non-existent things can be said to possess any properties at all, on this definition, a non-existent God would resemble an existent God more closely than the color red would resemble him. Hence, a non-existent God would, if anything, be more perfect than the property of being red which exists necessarily.

III. St. Anselm's third ontological argument

(1) If it is possible that x exists but in fact x does not exist, then it is possible that x comes into existence.

(2) It is possible that God exists.

(3) It is not possible that God comes into existence.

∴(4) Either it is not possible that God exists, or God exists. (By (1) and (3))

∴(5) God exists. (By (2) and 4))

Although the argument is valid, its first premiss is false. Let x be the eternal monster of Loch Ness. Now it is true that:

(α) It is possible that there exists the eternal monster of Loch Ness, although it is false that such a monster exists.

But it is false that:

(β) It is possible that the eternal monster of Loch Ness comes into existence.

It is false that it is possible for the eternal monster of Loch Ness to come into existence because an eternal being is, by definition, a being which cannot come into existence and cannot go out of existence. Because (α) is true and (β) is false, premiss (1) is false.

IV. St. Anselm's fourth ontological argument

(1) If a being than whom no greater can be conceived does not exist, then a being than whom no greater can be conceived is not a being than whom no greater can be conceived (for a greater can be conceived, namely, one that exists).

(2) The consequent of (1) is self-contradictory.

∴(3) A being than whom no greater can be conceived exists.

The argument is vitiated by the fact that either (2) is false, in which case the conclusion is not proved true; or the conclusion is the trivial tautology: Either God exists or God does not exist, which needs no proof and is not what the ontological argument is meant to prove anyway.

The second premiss, (2), is false; that is, the consequent of (1) is not self-contradictory, if we adopt its modern interpretation. The consequent of (1) says:

> (i) A being than whom no greater can be conceived is not a being than whom no greater can be conceived,

and this would be normally understood as saying that:

> (ii) All beings than whom no greater can be conceived are not beings than whom no greater can be conceived.

Modern logicians would read it as:

> (iii) If anything is a being than whom no greater can be conceived, then it is not a being than whom no greater can be conceived.

But (iii) is not self-contradictory. It is equivalent to the proposition:

> (iv) There are no beings than whom no greater can be conceived.

(iv) may be false, but it is not self-contradictory. Hence, if we adopt the modern interpretation of (ii), premiss (2) is false.

But another interpretation is possible. Traditional logicians, following Aristotle, read (ii) as:

> (v) There are beings than whom no greater can be conceived and every one of them is not a being than whom no greater can be conceived.

Now (v) is self-contradictory, which we can see easily enough.

> (vi) Every being than whom no greater can be conceived is not a being than whom no greater can be conceived.

is equivalent to:

> (vii) It is not the case that there are beings than whom no greater can be conceived.

Hence, (v) is the conjunction of (vii) and the denial of (vii), and such a conjunction is self-contradictory. To assure the truth of (2) we must assume that St. Anselm is interpreting (ii) in the traditional way.

And now we are committed to interpreting every statement in the argument of the form:

All *A*'s are *B*'s

in the traditional way. Accordingly, the antecedent of (1) is equivalent to:

(viii) There exist beings than whom no greater can be conceived and none of them exists.

But this is a flagrant self-contradiction. To be sure, the fact that the antecedent of (1), namely, (viii), is self-contradictory makes (1) true without further ado. For, a conditional statement whose antecedent is false is true. But this is to secure the truth of (1) at the price of vitiating the argument. For, now the conclusion of the argument is the trivial tautology:

(ix) Either a being than whom no greater can be conceived exists or it is not the case that a being than whom no greater can be conceived exists.

Propositions like (ix) are too obvious to need proving, and, anyway, the aim of the ontological argument is to prove a quite different proposition.

The antecedent of (1) is supposed to be what the atheist asserts. The ontological argument is offered as proof of the falsity of what the atheist asserts. But if what the atheist asserts is a blatant self-contradiction, it would be strange that philosophers should have invented arguments trying to prove it. In fact, the atheist's assertion is not self-contradictory, though it may be false, and it may even be necessarily false. Not all necessarily false propositions are self-contradictory. By so interpreting the premises of the present version of the ontological argument as to make them true, we trivialize the whole argument and force it to miss its mark.

PSYCHOLOGICAL PREDICATES

HILARY PUTNAM

The typical concerns of the Philosopher of Mind might be represented by three questions: (1) How do we know that other people have pains? (2) Are pains brain states? (3) What is the analysis of the concept *pain*? I do not wish to discuss questions (1) and (3) in this paper. I shall say something about question (2).[1]

I. Identity questions

"Is pain a brain state?" (Or, "Is the property of having a pain at time *t* a brain state?")[2] It is impossible to discuss this question sensibly without saying something about the peculiar rules which have grown up in the course of the development of "analytical philosophy"—rules which, far from leading to an end to all conceptual confusions, themselves represent considerable conceptual confusion. These rules—which are, of course, implicit rather than explicit in the practice of most analytical philosophers—are (1) that a statement of the form "being A is being B" (e.g.,"being in pain is being in a certain brain state") can be *correct* only if it follows, in some sense, from the meaning of the terms A and B; and (2) that a statement of the form "being A is being B" can be philosophically *informative* only if it is in some sense reductive (e.g. "being in pain is having a certain unpleasant sensation" is not philosophically informative; "being in pain is having a certain behavior disposition" is, if true, philosophically informative). These rules are excellent rules if we still believe that the program of reductive analysis (in the style of the 1930's) can be carried out; if we don't, then they turn analytical philosophy into a mug's game, at least so far as "is" questions are concerned.

In this paper I shall use the term 'property' as a blanket term for such things as being in pain, being in a particular brain state,

---

[1] I have discussed these and related topics in the following papers: "Minds and Machines," in *Dimensions of Mind*, ed. Sidney Hook, New York, 1960, pp. 148-179; "Brains and Behavior," in *Analytical Philosophy, second series*, ed. Ronald Butler, Oxford, 1965, pp. 1-20; and "The Mental Life of Some Machines," to appear in a volume edited by Hector Neri Castaneda, Detroit.

[2] In this paper I wish to avoid the vexed question of the relation between *pains* and *pain states*. I only remark in passing that one common argument *against* identification of these two—viz., that a pain can be in one's arm but a state (of the organism) cannot be in one's arm—is easily seen to be fallacious.

having a particular behavior disposition, and also for magnitudes such as temperature, etc.—i.e., for things which can naturally be represented by one-or-more-place predicates or functors. I shall use the term 'concept' for things which can be identified with synonymy-classes of expressions. Thus the concept *temperature* can be identified (I maintain) with the synonymy-class of the word 'temperature.'[3] (This is like saying that the number 2 can be identified with the class of all pairs. This is quite a different statement from the peculiar statement that 2 *is* the class of all pairs. I do not maintain that concepts *are* synonymy-classes, whatever that might mean, but that they can be identified with synonymy-classes, for the purpose of formalization of the relevant discourse.)

The question "What is the concept *temperature*?" is a very "funny" one. One might take it to mean "What is temperature? Please take my question as a conceptual one." In that case an answer might be (pretend for a moment 'heat' and 'temperature' are synonyms) "temperature is heat," or even "the concept of temperature is the same concept as the concept of heat." Or one might take it to mean "What are *concepts*, really? For example, what is 'the concept of temperature'?" In that case heaven knows what an "answer" would be. (Perhaps it would be the statement that concepts *can be identified with* synonymy-classes.)

Of course, the question "What is the property temperature?" is also "funny." And one way of interpreting it is to take it as a question about the concept of temperature. But this is not the way a physicist would take it.

The effect of saying that the property P_1 can be identical with the property P_2 only if the terms P_1, P_2 are in some suitable sense "synonyms" is, to all intents and purposes, to collapse the two notions of "property" and "concept" into a single notion. The view that concepts (intensions) *are* the same as properties has been explicitly advocated by Carnap (e.g., in *Meaning and Necessity*). This seems an unfortunate view, since "temperature is mean

---

[3] There are some well-known remarks by Alonzo Church on this topic. Those remarks do not bear (as might at first be supposed) on the identification of concepts with synonymy-classes as such, but rather support the view that (in formal semantics) it is necessary to retain Frege's distinction between the normal and the "oblique" use of expressions. That is, even if we say that the concept of temperature *is* the synonymy-class of the word 'temperature,' we must not thereby be led into the error of supposing that 'the concept of temperature' is synonymous with 'the synonymy-class of the word "temperature" '—for then 'the concept of temperature' and 'der Begriff der Temperatur' would not be synonymous, which they are. Rather, we must say that 'the concept of temperature' *refers to* the synonymy-class of the word 'temperature' (on this particular reconstruction); but that class is *identified* not as "the synonymy class to which such-and-such a word belongs," but in another way (e.g., as the synonymy-class whose members have such-and-such a characteristic use).

molecular kinetic energy" appears to be a perfectly good example of a true statement of identity of properties, whereas "the concept of temperature is the same concept as the concept of mean molecular kinetic energy" is simply false.

Many philosophers believe that the statement "pain is a brain state" violates some rules or norms of English. But the arguments offered are hardly convincing. For example, if the fact that I can know that I am in pain without knowing that I am in brain state S shows that pain cannot be brain state S, then, by exactly the same argument, the fact that I can know that the stove is hot without knowing that the mean molecular kinetic energy is high (or even that molecules exist) shows that it is *false* that temperature is mean molecular kinetic energy, physics to the contrary. In fact, all that immediately follows from the fact that I can know that I am in pain without knowing that I am in brain state S is that the concept of pain is not the same concept as the concept of being in brain state S. But either pain, or the state of being in pain, or some pain, or some pain state, might still be brain state S. After all, the concept of temperature is not the same concept as the concept of mean molecular kinetic energy. But temperature is mean molecular kinetic energy.

Some philosophers maintain that both 'pain is a brain state' and 'pain states are brain states' are unintelligible. The answer is to explain to these philosophers, as well as we can, given the vagueness of all scientific methodology, what sorts of considerations lead one to make an empirical reduction (i.e., to say such things as "water is H_2O," "light is electro-magnetic radiation," "temperature is mean molecular kinetic energy"). If, without giving reasons, he still maintains in the face of such examples that one cannot imagine parallel circumstances for the use of 'pains are brain states' (or, perhaps, 'pain states are brain states') one has grounds to regard him as perverse.

Some philosophers maintain that "P_1 is P_2" is something that can be true, when the 'is' involved is the 'is' of empirical reduction, only when the properties P_1 and P_2 are (a) associated with a spatio-temporal region; and (b) the region is one and the same in both cases. Thus "temperature is mean molecular kinetic energy" is an admissible empirical reduction, since the temperature and the molecular energy are associated with the same space-time region, but "having a pain in my arm is being in a brain state" is not, since the spatial regions involved are different.

This argument does not appear very strong. Surely no one is going to be deterred from saying that mirror images are light reflected from an object and then from the surface of a mirror by the fact that an image can be "located" three feet *behind* the mirror! (Moreover, one can always find *some* common property of the reductions one is willing to allow—e.g., temperature is mean molecular kinetic energy—which is not a property of some one identification one wishes to disallow. This is not very impressive unless one has an argument to show that the very purposes of such identification depend upon the common property in question.)

Again, other philosophers have contended that all the predictions that can be derived from the conjunction of neurophysiological laws with such statements as "pain states are such-and-such brain states" can equally well be derived from the conjunction of the same neurophysiological laws with "being in pain is correlated with such-and-such brain states," and hence (sic!) there can be no methodological grounds for saying that pains (or pain states) *are* brain states, as opposed to saying that they are *correlated* (invariantly) with brain states. This argument, too, would show that light is only correlated with electromagnetic radiation. The mistake is in ignoring the fact that, although the theories in question may indeed lead to the same predictions, they open and exclude different *questions*. "Light is invariantly correlated with electromagnetic radiation" would leave open the questions "What is the light then, if it isn't the same as the electromagnetic radiation?" and "What makes the light accompany the electromagnetic radiation?"—questions which are excluded by saying that the light *is* the electromagnetic radiation. Similarly, the purpose of saying that pains are brain states is precisely to exclude from empirical meaningfulness the questions "What is the pain, then, if it isn't the same as the brain state?" and "What makes the pain accompany the brain state?" If there are grounds to suggest that these questions represent, so to speak, the wrong way to look at the matter, then those grounds are grounds for a theoretical identification of pains with brain states.

If all arguments to the contrary are unconvincing, shall we then conclude that it is meaningful (and perhaps true) to say either that pains are brain states or that pain states are brain states?

(1) It is perfectly meaningful (violates no "rule of English," involves no "extension of usage") to say "pains are brain states."

(2) It is not meaningful (involves a "changing of meaning" or "an extension of usage," etc.) to say "pains are brain states."

My own position is not expressed by either (1) or (2). It seems to me that the notions "change of meaning" and "extension of usage" are simply so ill-defined that one cannot in fact say *either* (1) or (2). I see no reason to believe that either the linguist, or the man-on-the-street, or the philosopher possesses today a notion of "change of meaning" applicable to such cases as the one we have been discussing. The *job* for which the notion of change of meaning was developed in the history of the language was just a *much* cruder job than this one.

But, if we don't assert either (1) or (2)—in other words, if we regard the "change of meaning" issue as a pseudo-issue in this case—then how are we to discuss the question with which we started? "Is pain a brain state?"

The answer is to allow statements of the form "pain is A," where 'pain' and 'A' are in no sense synonyms, and to see whether any such statement can be found which might be acceptable on empirical and methodological grounds. This is what we shall now proceed to do.

II. Is pain a brain state?

We shall discuss "Is pain a brain state?," then. And we have agreed to waive the "change of meaning" issue.

Since I am discussing not what the concept of pain comes to, but what pain is, in a sense of 'is' which requires empirical theory-construction (or, at least, empirical speculation), I shall not apologize for advancing an empirical hypothesis. Indeed, my strategy will be to argue that pain is *not* a brain state, not on a *priori* grounds, but on the grounds that another hypothesis is more plausible. The detailed development and verification of my hypothesis would be just as Utopian a task as the detailed development and verification of the brain-state hypothesis. But the putting-forward, not of detailed and scientifically "finished" hypotheses, but of schemata for hypotheses, has long been a function of philosophy. I shall, in short, argue that pain is not a brain state, in the sense of a physical-chemical state of the brain (or even the whole nervous system), but another *kind* of state entirely. I propose the hypothesis that pain, or the state of being in pain, is a functional state of a whole organism.

To explain this it is necessary to introduce some technical notions. In previous papers I have explained the notion of a Turing Machine and discussed the use of this notion as a model for an organism. The notion of a Probabilistic Automaton is defined similarly to a Turing Machine, except that the transitions between "states" are allowed to be with various probabilities rather than being "deterministic." (Of course, a Turing Machine is simply a special kind of Probabilistic Automaton, one with transition probabilities 0, 1.) I shall assume the notion of a Probabilistic Automaton has been generalized to allow for "sensory inputs" and "motor outputs"—that is, the Machine Table specifies, for every possible combination of a "state" and a complete set of "sensory inputs," an "instruction" which determines the probability of the next "state," and also the probabilities of the "motor outputs."

(This replaces the idea of the Machine as printing on a tape.) I shall also assume that the physical realization of the sense organs responsible for the various inputs, and of the motor organs, is specified, but that the "states" and the "inputs" themselves are, as usual, specified only "implicitly"—i.e., by the set of transition probabilities given by the Machine Table.

Since an empirically given system can simultaneously be a "physical realization" of many different Probabilistic Automata, I introduce the notion of a *Description* of a system. A Description of S where S is a system, is any true statement to the effect that S possesses distinct states $S_1, S_2, \ldots, S_n$ which are related to one another and to the motor outputs and sensory inputs by the transition probabilities given in such-and-such a Machine Table. The Machine Table mentioned in the Description will then be called the Functional Organization of S relative to that Description, and the S_i such that S is in state S_i at a given time will be called the Total State of S (at that time) relative to that Description. It should be noted that knowing the Total State of a system relative to a Description involves knowing a good deal about how the system is likely to "behave," given various combinations of sensory inputs, but does *not* involve knowing the physical realization of the S_i as, e.g., physical-chemical states of the brain. The S_i, to repeat, are specified only *implicitly* by the Description—i.e., specified *only* by the set of transition probabilities given in the Machine Table.

The hypothesis that "being in pain is a functional state of the organism" may now be spelled out more exactly as follows:

(1) All organisms capable of feeling pain are Probabilistic Automata.

(2) Every organism capable of feeling pain possesses at least one Description of a certain kind (i.e., being capable of feeling pain *is* possessing an appropriate kind of Functional Organization).

(3) No organism capable of feeling pain possesses a decomposition into parts which separately possess Descriptions of the kind referred to in (2).

(4) For every Description of the kind referred to in (2), there exists a subset of the sensory inputs such that an organism with that Description is in pain when and only when some of its sensory inputs are in that subset.

This hypothesis is admittedly vague, though surely no vaguer than the brain-state hypothesis in its present form. For example, one would like to know more about the kind of Functional Organization that an organism must have to be capable of feeling pain, and more about the marks that distinguish the subset of the sensory inputs referred to in (4). With respect to the first question, one can probably say that the Functional Organization must include something that resembles a "preference function," or at least a preference partial ordering, and something that resembles an "inductive logic" (i.e., the Machine must be able to "learn from experience"). (The meaning of these conditions, for Automata models, is discussed in my paper "The Mental Life of Some Machines.") In addition, it seems natural to require that the Machine possess "pain sensors," i.e., sensory organs which normally signal damage to the Machine's body, or dangerous temperatures, pressures, etc., which transmit a special subset of the inputs, the subset referred to in (4). Finally, and with respect to the second question, we would want to require at least that the inputs in the distinguished subset have a high disvalue on the Machine's preference function or ordering (further conditions are discussed in "The Mental Life of Some Machines"). The purpose of condition (3) is to rule out such "organisms" (if they can count as such) as swarms of bees as single pain-feelers. The condition (1) is, obviously, redundant, and is only introduced for expository reasons. (It is, in fact, empty, since everything is a Probabilistic Automaton under *some* Description.)

I contend, in passing, that this hypothesis, in spite of its admitted vagueness, is far *less* vague than the "physical-chemical state" hypothesis is today, and far more susceptible to investigation of both a mathematical and an empirical kind. Indeed, to investigate this hypothesis is just to attempt to produce "mechanical" models of organisms—and isn't this, in a sense, just what psychology is about? The difficult step, of course, will be to pass from models of *specific* organisms to a *normal form* for the psychological description of organisms—for this is what is required to make (2) and (4) precise. But this too seems to be an inevitable part of the program of psychology.

I shall now compare the hypothesis just advanced with (a) the hypothesis that pain is a brain state, and (b) the hypothesis that pain is a behavior disposition.

III. Functional state versus brain state

It may, perhaps, be asked if I am not somewhat unfair in taking the brain-state theorist to be talking about *physical-chemical* states of the brain. But (a) these are the only sorts of states ever mentioned by brain-state theorists. (b) The brain-state theorist usually mentions (with a certain pride, slightly reminiscent of the Village Atheist) the incompatibility of his hypothesis with all forms of dualism and mentalism. This is natural if physical-chemical states of the brain are what is at issue. However, functional states of whole systems are something quite different. In particular, the functional-state hypothesis is *not* incompatible with dualism! Although it goes without saying that the hypothesis is "mechanistic" in its inspiration, it is a slightly remarkable fact that a system consisting of a body and a "soul," if such things there be, can perfectly well be a Probabilistic Automaton. (c) One argument advanced by Smart is that the brain-state theory assumes only "physical" properties, and Smart finds "non-physical" properties unintelligible. The Total States and the "inputs" defined above are, of course, neither mental nor physical *per se*, and I cannot imagine a functionalist advancing this argument. (d) If the brain-state theorist does mean (or at least allow) states other than physical-chemical states, then his hypothesis is completely empty, at least until he specifies *what* sort of "states" he *does* mean.

Taking the brain-state hypothesis in this way, then, what reasons are there to prefer the functional-state hypothesis over the brain-state hypothesis? Consider what the brain-state theorist has to do to make good his claims. He has to specify a physical-chemical state such that *any* organism (not just a mammal) is in pain if and only if (a) it possesses a brain of a suitable physical-chemical structure; and (b) its brain is in that physical-chemical state. This means that the physical-chemical state in question must be a possible state of a mammalian brain, a reptilian brain, a mollusc's brain (octopuses are mollusca, and certainly feel pain), etc. At the same time, it must *not* be a possible (physically possible) state of the brain of any physically possible creature that cannot feel pain. Even if such a state can be found, it must be nomologically certain that it will also be a state of the brain of any extra-terrestrial life that may be found that will be capable of feeling pain before we can even entertain the supposition that it may *be* pain.

It is not altogether impossible that such a state will be found. Even though octopus and mammal are examples of parallel (rather than sequential) evolution, for example, virtually identical structures (physically speaking) have evolved in the eye of the octopus and in the eye of the mammal, notwithstanding the fact that this organ has evolved from different kinds of cells in the two cases. Thus it is at least possible that parallel evolution, all over the universe, might *always* lead to *one and the same* physical "correlate" of pain. But this is certainly an ambitious hypothesis.

Finally, the hypothesis becomes still more ambitious when we realize that the brain state theorist is not just saying that *pain* is a brain state; he is, of course, concerned to maintain that *every* psychological state is a brain state. Thus if we can find even one psychological predicate which can clearly be applied to both a mammal and an octopus (say "hungry"), but whose physical-chemical "correlate" is different in the two cases, the brain-state theory has collapsed. It seems to me overwhelmingly probable that we can do this. Granted, in such a case the brain-state theorist can save himself by *ad hoc* assumptions (e.g., defining the disjunction of two states to be a single "physical-chemical state"), but this does not have to be taken seriously.

Turning now to the considerations *for* the functional-state theory, let us begin with the fact that we identify organisms as in pain, or hungry, or angry, or in heat, etc., on the basis of their *behavior*. But it is a truism that similarities in the behavior of two systems are at least a reason to suspect similarities in the functional organization of the two systems, and a much *weaker* reason to suspect similarities in the actual physical details. Moreover, we expect the various psychological states—at least the basic ones, such as hunger, thirst, aggression, etc.—to have more or less similar "transition probabilities" (within wide and ill-defined limits, to be sure) with each other and with behavior in the case of different species, because this is an artifact of the way in which we identify these states. Thus, we would not count an animal as *thirsty* if its "unsatiated" behavior did not seem to be directed toward drinking and was not followed by "satiation for liquid." Thus any animal that we count as capable of these various states will at least *seem* to have a certain rough kind of functional organization. And, as already remarked, if the program of finding psychological laws that are not species-specific—i.e., of finding a normal form for psychological theories of different species—ever succeeds, then it will bring in its wake a delineation of the kind of functional organization that is necessary and sufficient for a given psychological state, as well as a precise definition of the notion "psychological state." In contrast, the brain-state theorist has to hope for the eventual development of neurophysiological laws that are species-independent, which seems much less reasonable than the hope that psychological laws (of a sufficiently general kind) may be species-independent, or, still weaker, that a species-independent *form* can be found in which psychological laws can be written.

IV. Functional state versus behavior-disposition

The theory that being in pain is neither a brain state nor a functional state but a behavior disposition has one apparent advantage: it appears to agree with the way in which we verify that organisms are in pain. We do not in practice know anything about the brain state of an animal when we say that it is in pain; and we possess little if any knowledge of its functional organization, except in a crude intuitive way. In fact, however, this "advantage" is no advantage at all: for, although statements about how we verify that *x* is *A* may have a good deal to do with what the concept of being *A* comes to, they have precious little to do with what the property *A is*. To argue on the ground just mentioned that pain is neither a brain state nor a functional state is like arguing that heat is not mean molecular kinetic energy from the fact that ordinary people do not (they think) ascertain the mean molecular kinetic energy of something when they verify that it is hot or cold. It is not necessary that they should; what is necessary is that the marks that they take as indications of heat should in fact be explained by the mean molecular kinetic energy. And, similarly, it is necessary to our hypothesis that the marks that are taken as behavioral indications of pain should be explained by the fact that the organism is in a functional state of the appropriate kind, but not that speakers should *know* that this is so.

The difficulties with "behavior disposition" accounts are so well known that I shall do little more than recall them here. The difficulty—it appears to be more than "difficulty," in fact—of specifying the required behavior disposition except as "the disposition of *X* to behave as if *X* were in *pain*," is the chief one, of course. In contrast, we *can* specify the functional state with which we propose to identify pain, at least roughly, without using the notion of pain. Namely, the functional state we have in mind is the state of receiving sensory inputs which play a certain role in the Functional Organization of the organism. This role is characterized, at least partially, by the fact that the sense organs responsible for the inputs in question are organs whose function is to detect damage to the body, or dangerous extremes of temperature, pressure, etc., and by the fact that the "inputs" themselves, whatever their physical realization, represent a condition that the organism assigns a high disvalue to. As I stressed in "The Mental Life of Some Machines," this does *not* mean that the Machine will always *avoid* being in the condition in question ("pain"); it only means that the condition will be avoided unless not avoiding it is necessary to the attainment of some more highly valued goal. Since the behavior of the Machine (in this case, an organism) will depend not merely on the sensory inputs, but also on the Total State (i.e., on other values, beliefs, etc.), it seems hopeless to make any general statement about how an organism in such a condition *must* behave; but this does not mean that we must abandon hope of characterizing the condition. Indeed, we have just characterized it.[4]

[4] In "The Mental Life of Some Machines" a further, and somewhat independent, characteristic of the pain inputs is discussed in terms of Automata models—namely the spontaneity of the inclination to withdraw the injured part, etc. This raises the question, which is discussed in that paper, of giving a functional analysis of the notion of a spontaneous inclination. Of course, still further characteristics come readily to mind—for example, that feelings of pain are (or seem to be) *located* in the parts of the body.

Not only does the behavior-disposition theory seem hopelessly vague; if the "behavior" referred to is peripheral behavior, and the relevant stimuli are peripheral stimuli (e.g., we do not say anything about what the organism will do if its brain is operated upon), then the theory seems clearly false. For example, two animals with all motor nerves cut will have the same actual and potential "behavior" (viz., none to speak of); but if one has cut pain fibers and the other has uncut pain fibers, then one will feel pain and the other won't. Again, if one person has cut pain fibers, and another suppresses all pain responses deliberately due to some strong compulsion, then the actual and potential peripheral behavior may be the same, but one will feel pain and the other won't. (Some philosophers maintain that this last case is conceptually impossible, but the only evidence for this appears to be that *they* can't, or don't want to, conceive of it.)[5] If, instead of pain, we take some sensation the "bodily expression" of which is easier to suppress—say, a slight coolness in one's left little finger—the case becomes even clearer.

Finally, even if there *were* some behavior disposition invariantly correlated with pain (species-independently!), and specifiable without using the term 'pain,' it would still be more plausible to identify being in pain with some state whose presence *explains* this behavior disposition—the brain state or functional state—than with the behavior disposition itself. Such considerations of plausibility may be somewhat subjective; but if other things *were* equal (of course, they aren't) why shouldn't we allow considerations of plausibility to play the deciding role?

V. Methodological considerations

So far we have considered only what might be called the "empirical" reasons for saying that being in pain is a functional state, rather than a brain state or a behavior disposition; viz., that it seems more likely that the functional state we described is invariantly "correlated" with pain, species-independently, than that there is either a physical-chemical state of the brain (must an organism have a *brain* to feel pain? perhaps some ganglia will do) or a behavior disposition so correlated. If this is correct, then it follows that the identification we proposed is at least a candidate for consideration. What of methodological considerations?

The methodological considerations are roughly similar in all cases of reduction, so no surprises need be expected here. First, identification of psychological states with functional states means

[5] Cf. the discussion of "super-spartans" in "Brains and Behavior."

that the laws of psychology can be derived from statements of the form "such-and-such organisms have such-and-such Descriptions" together with the identification statements ("being in pain is such-and-such a functional state," etc.). Secondly, the presence of the functional state (i.e., of inputs which play the role we have described in the Functional Organization of the organism) is not merely "correlated with" but actually explains the pain behavior on the part of the organism. Thirdly, the identification serves to exclude questions which (if a naturalistic view is correct) represent an altogether wrong way of looking at the matter, e.g., "What *is* pain if it isn't either the brain state or the functional state?" and "What causes the pain to be always accompanied by this sort of functional state?" In short, the identification is to be tentatively accepted as a theory which leads to both fruitful predictions and to fruitful *questions*, and which serves to discourage fruitless and empirically senseless questions, where by 'empirically senseless' I mean "senseless" not merely from the standpoint of verification, but from the standpoint of what there in fact *is*.

COMMENTS

BRUCE AUNE

I want to begin by expressing my admiration for Professor Putnam's sophisticated paper. As my comments will show, I disagree strongly with some of his conclusions, but I nevertheless think that his paper as a whole marks an important advance in our understanding of the topics it treats.

Early in his paper (pp. 38-39) Putnam attacks the principle that properties can correctly be regarded as identical only if their corresponding predicates are in some sense synonymous. There are two features of this attack on which I want to make a brief comment. First, he claims that this principle implies that concepts and properties are "to all intents and purposes" identical, that, for example, pain and the concept of pain are the same. I am not sure exactly what he packs into the idea of "to all intents and purposes," but I am sure that he has not in any way demonstrated that this bizarre implication holds. All that does follow, so far as I can tell, from the conjunction of his definition of concepts as synonymy-classes of expressions and the principle he attacks is that if the properties *pain* and, say, *brain state X* are identical, then the concept of pain is identical with the concept of that brain state; it does *not* follow that the concept of pain is identical with pain itself.

Now, Putnam would no doubt want to argue that even if the synonymy principle for predicates did not imply the identity of pain and the concept of pain, it could still be seen to be untenable in virtue of the implication that does hold, namely that if pain is the same property as a certain brain state, then the concept of pain would have to be identical with the concept of that brain state. He would regard this as an untenable consequence because while he is fully confident that the concept of pain is *not* the concept of a brain state, he thinks it is at least an open question, an empirical one, whether the property *pain* is or is not identical with the property, say, *brain state X*. In support of this last belief, namely that *pain* and *brain state X* might possibly be identical as properties, he cites a number of familiar theoretical identity statements, such as "Water is H_2O," and argues that these are not only the same sort of thing as the statement identifying *pain* and *brain state X*, but also that there are good grounds for regarding them as empirical, true, and important.

D 49

I think this last move of Putnam's is a bit disingenuous, for he knows full well that the theoretical identity statements he cites are extremely problematic, leading to some of the most basic and hard-fought problems in the philosophy of science, especially those associated with the notion of a correspondence rule. Later on in my comments I shall have something to say on the subject of theoretical identity statements, but for the moment I shall restrict myself to the remark that the problematic character of such identity statements is *far too great* to support a *reductio ad absurdum* of the synonymy principle he mentions. For the fact is, what he regards as an out-and-out absurdity is regarded by others, often with very good reason, as a profound grain of wisdom.

Having argued that theoretical identifications are both sound and important, Putnam announces his task (p. 41) as that of showing that pains are *not* brain states, because the hypothesis that they are functional states is more probable. By his own later admission, however, this inference is unwarranted, for it turns out that the functional-state hypothesis is *not* inconsistent with the brain-state hypothesis. The reason for this is that the functional-state hypothesis characterizes pain in a way that is essentially formal, and in so doing, it does not, as Putnam admits, rule out any hypothesis as to the empirical features of that state, that is, whether its empirical "realization" is physical, mental, or whatever. Putnam does, it is true, attempt to cast serious doubt on the brain state hypothesis, but he does this only by showing that it is extremely risky, and that we should do better not to commit ourselves to more than the functional-state hypothesis for a long time to come. His sympathies, nevertheless, still *seem* to lie with the idea that the empirical features of the functional state "identified with" pain will be physical, though perhaps not every functional state filling the bill for pain will have exactly the same physical features. It is perhaps worth noting that if this latter idea is sound, the physicalist might still feel that his metaphysical battle is won; for he would be quite content, I think, if he were assured that the functional state "identified with" pain would always have a purely physical "realization"—indeed, this assurance would entitle him to assert that every pain is identical with some brain state or other.

Toward the end of his paper, Putnam remarks that when functional states have a purely physical realization, they are not themselves physical states, any more than the trajectory of a particle is itself a particle. Assuming that this is so, are we then strictly entitled to say that some functional states are pains? An affirmative answer here sounds just as dubious as an affirmative answer to "Are some functional states brain states?" The reason for this dubiousness, I submit, is that the sense in which a pain may be said to *be* a functional state is very different from the sense in which, to take Putnam's example, water may be said to *be* H_2O. Consider in this connection the remark, "Those pennies and nickels are pawns and knights in the particular chess game those men are playing." What could be the force of such a remark? Using Putnam's language, I think the thing to say is this: "Those pennies and nickels serve, respectively, as the empirical realizations of the pawn-elements and the knight-elements in the functional organization of *that* game of chess."

The point here is that Putnam's functional-state hypothesis does not affirm an identity of the empirical, theoretical sort that is affirmed by such statements as "pains are modes of a Cartesian soul" or "pains are brain states." The functional-state hypothesis has, of course, certain similarities with these identity statements, one being that it is an empirical question as to whether the actual state that pain is, with its own peculiar empirical features, does or does not have the *formal* characteristics distinctive of a certain *functional* state. On the other hand, however, it will not (I take it) be an empirical question whether pain has the formal features distinctive of *some functional state or other*. As Putnam says, any complex empirical system can be regarded as a probabilistic automaton; and the states of any system will, by definition, be functional states.

Because the considerations that show that functional states are not (sometimes) physical states also show that they are not, in the same sense, feeling-pain states, it appears that Putnam's claim that he is advancing an empirical identification of a theoretical sort is false. I hasten to add, however, that one can still say that having a pain is being in a functional state; what one cannot say, if I am right, is that pain and the functional state can be theoretically identified by virtue of empirical considerations.

Before turning to empirical identities proper, I want to say something about a different sense in which Putnam *could* say that pain is strictly identical with a functional state. The sense I have in mind would be involved in the claim that the *concept* of pain is in fact the *concept* of a functional state. This claim, which I am not prepared to endorse but which I think is at least reasonable, would be true if Schlick were right when he said that our ordinary, intersubjective concepts of mental states can capture their form or structure, not their "content."[1] For if our ordinary concept of pain did not grasp the content qualities, or the intrinsic empirical features, of pain but only its structural aspects, then this concept would in effect *be* the concept of a functional state. In virtue of the synonymy

---

[1] Moritz Schlick, "Form and Content," *Gesammelte Aufsätze*, Vienna, 1938.

principle for properties mentioned earlier, it could then be argued, wholly on *a priori* grounds, that the property *pain* is identical with a certain functional property. This would give us the out-and-out identity statement that Putnam seems to be after—in fact, it would seem to be the *only way* of getting a strict identity of properties.

I turn now to a brief statement about empirical, theoretical identities properly so called. The first point to note is that the examples of such identities that Putnam cites—for instance, light is electromagnetic radiation, water is H_2O, temperature is mean molecular kinetic energy—all involve items having intrinsic empirical features. Now, the reason that these identities are so problematic is that the features built into the notion of one of the items of the identity-pair are not built into the other. For example, water is ordinarily conceived mainly with respect to observable properties (wetness, relative transparency, etc.) and these properties are not built into the notion of an agglomeration of H_2O molecules. Where an identity statement is of this type—where, that is, one term of the identity statement might be said to be "in the observation language" while the other might be said to be "in a theoretical language"—we are immediately face-to-face with all of the classical problems about correspondence rules; for the identity statement seems to connect items of radically different sorts, that is, they seem to identify perceptual objects or properties with purely theoretical ones. Yet nothing seems clearer to an unprejudiced eye than that the observable property ordinarily called "light" is very different from the rarefied theoretical property of electromagnetic radiation. In fact it is the apparently obvious difference of these properties that has done so much to tempt philosophers to defend the familiar double-levels picture of noninstantial theories, and to insist that there can be at best a correlation between theoretical and observable phenomena.

Now, like Putnam, I think that reductionism is untenable and that the "correlation view" of theoretical identity-statements must be abandoned. But this does not mean that I am prepared to identify common-sense perceptual properties with theoretical ones. On the contrary, what I want to say is that in so far as the identity statements he mentions are true and important, they involve the claim that the common sense items of the identity-pairs are to be *reconceived* in theoretical terms. As such, they imply that one notion, or one property, is to be regarded as *supplanting* the other for theoretical purposes.[2] To the extent that they are held to be true statements, they must therefore involve a redefinition of one of the terms

[2] On this point see William Kneale, *Probability and Induction*, Oxford, 1949, p. 96, and Wilfrid Sellars, "The Language of Theories," in his *Science, Perception, and Reality*, London, 1964, pp. 106-126.

involved. Let me put my point by reference to an example. Consider the theoretical identification of a red-hot piece of iron with a highly agitated aggregate of ferric molecules. Notice that the color of the iron is common-sensically conceived as an occurrent sensuous property, not as a disposition: it is, in other words, conceived in that "naive" way that has given philosophers so much trouble. Such a conception of color must, however, be metamorphosed a bit to fit in with the physicists's ideas of an aggregate of molecules; it might, for instance, be reconceived in Lockean terms. In any case, it is, I would say, *only because* of some such metamorphosis that the identity statement in point can be regarded as both true and important.

Transposing these remarks to the "pain is a brain state" hypothesis, I would maintain that if the hypothesis is not to be regarded as patently false, it must also involve a change in the meaning of the word 'pain.' (Let me emphasize at once that in my view this meaning-change would in no way *trivialize* the identity hypothesis: it *could* still be both true and important.) Now, Putnam expressed considerable doubt about the "precision" of the notion of a change in meaning, and for this reason alone is likely to object strongly to the tack I am taking here. But (a) he has certainly not *shown* that our notion of a change in meaning is too vague to handle the present case, and (b) he has himself unwittingly formulated an argument to show *why* the brain-state hypothesis *would* involve a change in the meaning of the word 'pain.' For in arguing that pain is at least formally a functional state, he has argued that it is a state of an organism *as a whole*, not (by his assertion 3) a state of a *part* of an organism. Since a brain *is* a part of an organism, not the organism itself, to regard pain as a state *of that part* is implicitly to change the concept of pain. In other words, in arguing (successfully, I believe) that the state that pain is has a formal structure such that it qualifies as a functional state of a unitary organism, he has implicitly shown that pain could not, as presently conceived, qualify as a state of a brain: its formal structure is alone sufficient to forestall such an identification.

Let me make one more point before I stop. Assume that I am right in my view that any worth while brain-state hypothesis would require some change in the meaning of the word 'pain.' Might such a hypothesis yet be true and important? Well, it goes without saying that it would be a risky one: as Feigl once put it, it is at best a "bold and risky guess."[3] But notice that even if empirical and methodological reasons could lead us to accept the hypothesis, it would not *follow* that the brain state in point would not involve

[3] Herbert Feigl, "The 'Mental' and the 'Physical'," in *Minnesota Studies in the Philosophy of Science*, Vol. 3, eds. H. Feigl *et al.*, Minneapolis, 1958, pp. 370-457.

peculiar "emergent" features, in the sense of 'emergent' discussed by Meehl and Sellars.[4] I throw out this last point—knowing I am throwing it feebly—for two reasons. First, if we are to get anywhere with the identity thesis, we shall need some clear criterion by which to distinguish physical from nonphysical phenomena. The notion of emergence, suitably clarified, might help to give us this criterion. Second, if we consider such cases as after-images—the sort, for instance, that one might naturally call "red and fuzzy-edged"—it would appear that any brain-state hypothesis could have plausibility only if the brain states in point could be understood as having some very peculiar phenomenal features; and this would be so even if the brain state is regarded as an "empirical realization" of a component, in some sense, of a complicated functional state of a unitary organism.

[4] P. E. Meehl and W. S. Sellars, "The Concept of Emergence," in *Minnesota Studies in Philosophy of Science*, Vol. 1, eds. H. Feigl and M. Scriven, Minneapolis, 1956, pp. 239-252.

COMMENTS

U. T. PLACE

When I was asked to comment on a paper by Putnam entitled "Psychological Predicates," I expected to find myself discussing a paper dealing with the problems of how far there is any characteristic or set of characteristics which distinguish psychological predicates from predicates of a non-psychological kind. I have always assumed, at least since first reading Ryle's *The Concept of Mind*, that mental or psychological predicates are an extremely heterogeneous collection and that any theory which purports to hold good for psychological predicates in general would be difficult to sustain.

I was therefore somewhat surprised to find not only that Putnam was confining his discussion to one very special kind of psychological predicate, namely 'pain' predicates, but also that he was apparently assuming that conclusions which are arguably true of pain statements can be readily extended to cover psychological predicates in general.

Putnam begins by distinguishing three typical questions which concern the philosopher of mind: "(1) How do we know that other people have pains? (2) Are pains brain states? (3) What is the analysis of the concept of pain?" He then says that he proposes to confine his discussion to the second of these questions. This is unfortunate. For had he devoted some time to the analysis of the concept of pain, he might have avoided discussing the relative merits of three theories about pains, namely that they are brain states, functional states, and behavioral dispositions, all three of which in my view are false—false because pains are not states and hence cannot be brain states, functional states, or behavioral dispositions.

Putnam refers to the theory he discusses according to which pains are brain states as a theory some philosophers have held. He does not say which philosophers; but one gathers from a reference to Smart at one point that he is referring to a view which I put forward in an article in the *British Journal of Psychology* in 1956 and which was defended by J. J. C. Smart in an article in *Philosophical Review* in 1959.[1] My thesis in that paper was not the thesis that statements

---

[1] U. T. Place, "Is Consciousness a Brain Process?," *British Journal of Psychology*, XLVII, 1956, pp. 44-50. J. J. C. Smart, "Sensations and Brain Processes," *Philosophical Review*, LXVIII, 1959, pp. 141-156. Both papers are republished in *The Philosophy of Mind*, ed. V. C. Chappell, Englewood Cliffs, New Jersey, 1962.

like "pain is a brain state" are logically defensible. I do not think they are and did not think so when I wrote the paper. The view I was defending and the view which Smart defends in his paper is that statements like "having a pain is a process in the brain" are logically defensible, and I emphasize the word 'process.' The theory as I understand it is a theory about mental processes, not a theory about mental states, and having a pain on this view is a mental process, not a mental state. And if it is not a mental state it cannot be a brain state.

It may be argued in Putnam's favor that there is a sense of 'state' in which having a pain is a state. We might say that being in pain is an unpleasant state to be in. Nevertheless we do not speak of having a pain as a state of mind. Being in pain can and usually does have devastating effects on an individual's state of mind, but it is not itself a state of mind. A state of mind is the sort of thing that Ryle[2] has called a short term tendency or disposition. Examples of states of mind are emotional states such as elation, depression, excitement, anger, fear, disgust, embarassment, jealousy, boredom, weariness, and nostalgia; moods of various kinds, such as reflective, cheerful, irritable, joking, and garrulous; short term propositional attitudes such as expecting, doubting, and intending; and abnormal states of consciousness such as confusion, disorientation, and delirium. States of mind are like mental processes and unlike mental capacities, traits of character, and other long-term tendencies and dispositions in that it is possible to distinguish fairly clearly defined periods of time during which they are and are not the case. And as Wittgenstein[3] has pointed out they share with mental processes the property of being continuously the case from their beginning to their end.

Mental states differ from mental processes, that is from sensations, experiences, thoughts, mental pictures, dreams, and the like, in that although they are continuously the case from their beginning to their end, they cannot be said to be continuously going on. It is this characteristic of being something of which it makes sense to say that it is going on continuously from its onset to its offset that differentiates mental processes[4] from other mental occurrences and conditions. It is closely connected with another logical feature of

[2] G. Ryle, *The Concept of Mind*, London, 1949, pp. 95-97.

[3] L. Wittgenstein, *Philosophical Investigations*, Oxford, 1953, p. 59, footnote (a).

[4] It will be appreciated that the term 'mental process' is being used here in a technical sense. In its ordinary use, in so far as it has one, the term 'mental process' is roughly equivalent to 'thinking' in the activity sense of that term. The use of a technical term to characterize this particular variety of mental occurrences seems unavoidable. There are a number of other technical terms to be found in the philosophical and psychological literature which embrace approximately the same range of concepts—'experience,' 'consciousness,' 'conscious experience,' 'sensations,' 'raw feels,' etc. All of them are in one way or another misleading.

mental processes, namely their logical connection with mental activity verbs. Thus for every expression in which an individual is said to have a mental process there is a corresponding verbal expression in which he can be said to do what he otherwise has, and the doing is an activity kind of doing. I can both have thoughts and think, have dreams and dream, have a mental picture and visualize, have a sensation and pay attention to it, and my thinking, dreaming, visualizing, and attending are all things I can be engaged in doing. Most mental states, on the other hand, are expressed in an adjectival rather than in a verbal form. They are things people are said to be or to be in, rather than things they have or do. And in the case of propositional attitude states where we *do* use the verbal form, where one can both have intentions and intend, have doubts and doubt, have expectations and expect, the verb is not an activity verb. Expecting, doubting, and intending are not things one can be engaged in doing.

Another difference between mental states and mental processes is that mental states are in an important sense less private than are mental processes. They are shown and expressed in behavior in a way that mental processes are not. I can express my intention or my anger, or show my confusion, or what I expect, in what I say or do. Philosophers often talk about the behavioral expressions of pain, as if pain was expressed in behavior in the way that anger is expressed. We might say "he expressed the pain he felt at this disappointment," using 'pain' in a derivative sense in which it serves to characterize a state of distress; but we never say "he expressed the pain he felt in his big toe." Nor do we say that he showed the pain in his toe. That sort of pain can't be shown. What we show in our behavior is *that* we are in pain. We betray the fact, we do not express it. True we can express our thoughts, but we do not express them in our behavior or in what we say—we express them in words.

If mental processes cannot be expressed in what we say and do in the way that mental states can, by the same token mental states cannot be described by their owner in the way that mental processes can. I can describe what it is or was like to have a particular sensation or experience, what my after images, mental pictures, or dreams are or were like. It makes no sense to ask me to describe what it is like to have an intention or to expect something. It makes some sense to ask me to describe what it was like to be angry or confused, but if you ask me to do so, what I describe are the sensations and thoughts that I had at the time, not the anger that was expressed or the confusion that was shown in my thoughts, in what I said and in my behavior.

The distinction between mental states and mental processes may seem a fine one, but it is a distinction which is vital to the theory of psycho-physical identity in the form in which I hold it. To explain why this is so, it may be helpful to say something about the reasons which originally led Smart and myself to formulate this view. I cannot speak for Feigl[5] here who came to hold a very similar view independently by a rather different route.

At the time when this thesis was being hammered into shape at the University of Adelaide, both Smart and myself were strongly influenced by Ryle and *The Concept of Mind*. Both of us, though for slightly different reasons, wanted to get rid of the notion of extra-physical mental states and processes.

We both thought that Ryle's dispositional theory had effectively and permanently knocked the ghost out of such concepts as "intelligence," "knowledge," "comprehension," "memory," "belief," and "motives"; but we were worried about the apparently irreducibly subjective character of another group of concepts clustering around the notions of "sensations," "dreams," and "mental images." We were aware of Wittgenstein's[6] attempt to reduce pain to pain behavior but were unconvinced by it, although Smart's adoption of the identity thesis was delayed by a feeling that it might somehow prove possible to develop a more defensible version of the Wittgensteinian view.

Admittedly we did not consider Putnam's functional-state theory in this connection, not merely, I think, because it was not then available, but because we did not think we needed a theory to do the job which in my view the functional-state theory does. As I see it, the functional-state theory is a theory designed to meet objections to a behavioral-disposition theory of mental states, capacities, and tendencies similar to those which Putnam outlines in his paper against a behavioral-disposition theory of pain. The objections to Ryle's dispositional theory of mental states, capacities, and tendencies are now well known, but in the early nineteen fifties they were only faint whispers and we did not seriously consider them. We were concerned not with the inadequacy of the dispositional theory in those cases where it appears at first sight to provide a reasonably plausible and convincing account, but with those cases where Ryle himself makes no attempt to apply it and, as in the case of sensation,[7] has to apologize for falling in with what he calls "the official story." And the reasons which led us (and Ryle presumably) to reject the dispositional account in the case of sensations, mental images, and dreams, namely their episodic and describable character, would, I am convinced, have led us to reject the functional-

---

[5] H. Feigl, "The 'Mental' and the 'Physical'," in *Minnesota Studies in the Philosophy of Sciences*, Vol. II, eds. H. Feigl *et al.*, Minneapolis, 1958, pp. 370-497.

[6] Wittgenstein, *op. cit.*, paragraphs 367, 370.

[7] Ryle, *op. cit.*, p. 200.

state theory as applied to these concepts had we considered it at the time. Certainly nothing that Putnam has said convinces me that the objections which convinced us that the dispositional theory of sensations will not do, do not apply with equal force to the functional-state theory.

I am conscious at this point that I may be overstating my case in that what I mean by a functional-state theory may not in fact be what Putnam means by a functional-state theory. Indeed I am inclined to think that there are two functional-state theories or, as I should prefer to call them, a functional-state theory and a functional-process theory, and that what is wrong with Putnam's paper is that he confuses the two. He is led into this confusion, I suggest, partly by a sense of the word 'state' in which it can quite properly be used to refer to the condition of continuous process at a specific point in time, the sort of thing that is caught by a still photograph of a moving object, and partly by the discontinuous step-like character of the operations carried out by the sort of electronic hardware on which his theoretical model is implicitly based, and in which it differs markedly from the continuous stream-like character of such biological processes as consciousness or the circulation of the blood. This confusion is reflected in his presentation of what I should prefer to call a functional-process theory of pain as an alternative to and hence, by implication, as incompatible with the psycho-physical identity thesis.

As I see it, it is not the functional-process theory which is incompatible with the psycho-physical identity thesis, but another theory, the functional-state theory proper. The functional-process theory, which is the sort of theory, I think, Putnam is trying to develop, can in principle be made to yield a valid account of pain and other mental processes. This theory, I shall argue, is in no way incompatible with and is in fact complementary to the psycho-physical identity theory. The functional-state theory proper, which *is* incompatible with psycho-physical identity, provides an excellent account of mental states, capacities, and tendencies; but it fails as an account of pain and other mental processes. Since, however, the psycho-physical identity theory is not intended to cover mental states, capacities, and tendencies, there is no conflict between the two theories provided each is restricted to its proper domain.

Since I am not as familiar as Putnam is with Turing machines and probabilistic automata and how one ought to talk about them, I propose, in stating the difference between these two theories to use the analogy of a machine that I do know how to talk about, namely, the automobile. Automobiles lack a great many features which human beings possess, but like any functioning system they have what I want to call functional states or performance characteristics and they have functional processes going on inside them, and these are different. A functional state in my sense is a performance characteristic like the car's horsepower. Performance characteristics like horsepower provide a very good conceptual analogy in my view not only for capacities like knowledge and intelligence, but also for tendencies like beliefs and motives. Like an individual's beliefs and motives a car's horsepower determines the way it behaves when driven in a way which it is not quite natural to describe as causal; and it is just about as implausible to suggest that horsepower statements are reducible to a complex set of hypothetical statements about how the car would behave in an indeterminate variety of situations as it is to say this about belief and motive statements.

It is less easy, perhaps, to find a convincing analogy for mental states in the automobile, since automobiles do not generally exhibit the phenomenon of spontaneous recovery from changes in their performance characteristics, apart from those, such as ease of starting, which vary with the weather. Nevertheless, it makes sense to talk of carbon deposits in the cylinder head or a dragging brake as altering the performance characteristics of the machine, even though these changes have no special names and cannot normally be reversed without recourse to surgery.

The important thing about functional states considered as performance characteristics of the machine is that they are characteristics of the whole functioning unit under consideration, and not of its individual parts. The performance characteristics depend, of course, on the physical dimensions and characteristics of the machine; but the horsepower is not the same thing as the constructional feature on which it depends. Clearly if we apply this analogy to mental states, capacities, and tendencies we do not want to say that they *are* the physical states of the brain microstructure. The most we could possibly want to claim is that they are characteristics of the individual as a functioning unit which he has by virtue of the current state of the microstructure of his brain.

Now there are some philosophers, and I am not altogether clear whether Putnam is one of these, who want to say that having a pain is a performance characteristic of the whole person and not of any one of its parts in the way that the horsepower of a car is a characteristic of the machine as a whole or at least of the engine as a whole and not of any of its individual parts. But if, as I have argued, having a pain is a process, this cannot be right. The only processes that can apply to the car as a whole are its actual movements, accelerating, turning corners, slowing down, etc. These surely correspond to the individual's overt behavior; and having a pain or a dream, with all due respect to the Wittgensteinians, is not primarily a matter of overt behavior. Nor does Putnam want to say that it is.

But if having a pain is a process and is not the overt behavior of the system as a whole, the only sort of process it can be is a process involving some specific part or parts of the controlling machinery. In terms of the automobile analogy, it must be, to use an example which I owe to Putnam himself in conversation, something like the pumping process which occurs in the car's fuel pump. Now it is perfectly true, as Putnam, I think, would want to point out, that we can specify this pumping process in terms of its functional properties in the total system without saying anything about its physical realization. We can characterize the pumping process in functional terms without knowing anything about the size or other physical characteristics of the actual pump involved and its precise physical location within the machine as a whole. But this does not mean that we cannot go on to ask what form the physical realization actually takes and where it is physically located. It always makes sense to ask what the physical realization and physical location of a functionally defined process are in a given case, in a way that it does not make sense to ask for a specification of the physical realization and physical location of a performance characteristic such as horsepower.

Furthermore, the functionally defined process and its physical realization are not two independent causally related things in the way that a performance characteristic and the structural characteristics on which it depends are two independent causally related things. It is true that the functional description of a process is only contingently related to the description of its physical realization. Fuel pumps differ in design and in the details of their construction, although they all have the same functional description in relation to the machine as a whole, and no conclusions about the design or position of the fuel pump of my car follow from the statement that it has one. But this does not mean that the physical description and the functional description refer to two different things, and no one but a Platonist would think that they did.

I have a great deal of sympathy with Putnam's attempt to construct a machine model in terms of which it is possible to specify in functional terms what is involved in someone's having a pain. Where I cannot agree with him is in claiming that his theory is an alternative hypothesis which is somehow incompatible with the psycho-physical identity hypothesis. I would prefer to regard this type of enterprise as one of the essential steps in a program designed to give some empirically testable substance to the psycho-physical identity hypothesis. I have spoken in the past[8] of the materialist

[8] U. T. Place, "Materialism as a Scientific Hypothesis," *Philosophical Review*, LXIX, 1960, pp. 101-104.

thesis as a scientific hypothesis, and I still believe that in an important sense this is right; but as it stands it is more in the nature of a
proposal or "schematon," to use Putnam's term, for the construction
of hypotheses than an actual hypothesis. We can see this if we ask
the Popperian question, "What evidence would count against it?"
Clearly, as it stands, we should have to know all that there is to know
about the brain before we could be certain that it contains nothing
which satisfies the logical criteria that have to be satisfied in order
for us to be able to say that this brain process is that mental process;
and how would we ever know that we knew all that there was to
know? Only when we can formulate hypotheses which assert the
identity of specific mental processes with specific brain processes,
do we have a genuine scientific theory which is susceptible to
empirical disconfirmation. And it is only when we begin to specify
in precise functional terms what sort of processes these might be,
that it becomes at all possible to make concrete suggestions as to
their possible physical realizations.

Our present situation is rather like that of a man who is trying to
work out from the way it performs, from the noises that it makes,
and from a superficial inspection of the working parts, how an
automobile works. Above the din of the motor he hears from time to
time what he identifies as a pumping noise and wants to know
where and what it is that is doing the pumping. He cannot locate
the sound because of the background noise and all he has to go on is
the hypothesis that there is some kind of pump operating. So he
follows Putnam and starts to construct a theory of how such a thing
as an automobile might work and what function a pump might have
in such a system. Once he hits on the notion that a system such as
this would require a pump to pump fuel from the fuel reservior
to the fuel injection system and can locate the fuel tank and fuel
injection system with a fair degree of certainty, he knows where to
look to find the fuel pump. But if he followed Putnam's advice he
would not attempt to locate the fuel pump for fear that his first
hypothesis might turn out to be wrong. He would have to remain
satisfied with the tantalizing knowledge that somewhere in the
machinery there must be one.

Putnam argues that one of the virtues of his theory, as compared
with the psycho-physical identity theory, is that it is consistent with
any number of possible theories about the nature of the physical
realization of pain conceived as a functional state, including dualism,
which he interprets as the view that pains "qua" functional states
have "transphysical realizations." I have two comments[9] to make

---

[9] I owe the suggestion that I should comment on this part of Putnam's paper to
Professor R. N. Smart.

about this contention. In the first place the psycho-physical identity theory considered as a philosophical thesis is no less consistent with any hypothesis about the physical realization of mental processes than is a theory such as Putnam's. For the psycho-physical identity theory considered as a philosophical thesis is not the thesis that sensations, etc., are brain processes; it is the thesis that this statement makes sense, not the thesis that it is true. What is maintained is that this is a scientific hypothesis which, like any scientific hypothesis, may turn out to be false.

We have already seen that there are problems in specifying the evidence which would constitute a decisive disconfirmation of the hypothesis. Nevertheless, supposing for the sake of argument that we did have good reasons for thinking that we had examined all the possible physical realizations in terms of brain activity that could conceivably be suggested, and shown that none of them satisfied the relevant criteria which would enable us to identify them as the sensations reported by the subject, we would then be forced to conclude that the hypothesis is false. And if the hypothesis, although sensible, is nevertheless false and there are no other physical processes which could conceivably be identified as the mental processes in question, we should then have no alternative but to conclude that some form of dualism must be true. How we could ever hope to formulate a dualistic hypothesis in such a way that it would become empirically disconfirmable, in the way that I have suggested the brain process hypothesis can and should be made empirically disconfirmable, is beyond me. This, however, is a problem that can safely be left until we find ourselves forced by the empirical evidence into the situation of having to adopt such a theory, a situation which is not likely to arise in the forseeable future, if it arises at all.

The fact that the psycho-physical identity thesis has the same implication in this respect as Putnam's functional-state or, as I should prefer to call it, functional-process theory strongly suggests that this theory is not so much an alternative to the psycho-physical identity thesis as another way of saying the same thing. But if so, and this brings me to my second comment, there is something wrong with Putnam's contention that the functional-state (process) theory is an empirical hypothesis. For it is only in the capacity of a philosophical thesis that the psycho-physical identity thesis is compatible with dualism, which would suggest that in so far as it is consistent with dualism the functional-state (process) theory is likewise a philosophical thesis rather than an empirical hypothesis. There is, in any case, something rather implausible about an alleged scientific hypothesis which is going to be right however the facts turn out. Immunity from empirical disconfirmation is not as

Putnam seems to think a virtue in a scientific theory, though it may be a virtue in a philosophical one.

What Putnam is doing, I suggest, is giving us an analysis or elucidation of the concept of pain in terms of a machine model. The facts which would count against his theory are not psychological facts or neurophysiological facts; they are logical or perhaps we should say linguistic facts, facts about the use of the word 'pain.' The theory he outlines in his paper is an account of what a machine would have to be like for us to be able to ascribe pain to it. And it is the contention implicit in this enterprise that machines are conceivable to which the concept of pain can be properly ascribed, which would appear to be logically equivalent to the contention of the psycho-physical identity theorist that statements like "having a pain is a brain process" makes sense.

For if it makes sense to ascribe pain to a mechanical system and the brain is such a system, as it clearly is, then it must make sense to ascribe pain to the brain. And as we have seen, to say that it makes sense to ascribe pain to the brain is not to say that pain actually *is* something going on in the brain, only that it may be.

The conclusion that Putnam is providing a conceptual elucidation of the concept of pain, rather than developing a scientific hypothesis, appears at first sight to have some embarrassing consequences. For if what he is doing in describing a machine to which the concept of "having a pain" could be properly ascribed, it would seem to follow that the only sense in which having a pain could be said to be the relevant functional state of the machine would be a sense in which this is analytically true. And to say this would be to say that the functional description means the same as the pain statement, which is plainly false.

I suggest that in order to defend the validity of Putnam's enterprise we need to draw a distinction between two things which I propose to call "a conceptual analysis" and "a conceptual elucidation." By "a conceptual analysis" I mean a set of statements which taken together jointly assert all that is asserted and only what is asserted by the *analysandum*. In this case the *analysans* is offered as a translation of the *analysandum*, and the meaning relation between them is symmetrical. The *analysans* expresses everything that the *analysandum* expresses and vice versa. It may be doubted whether there are any statements which are susceptible to conceptual analysis in this sense; but on any view there must be at least some that are not, and it seems very possible that pain statements are a case in point. It may nevertheless be the case that there are statements which are not susceptible to conceptual analysis, which are susceptible to what I want to call "conceptual elucidation." In doing what I call "conceptual elucidation" a piece of theoretical apparatus is constructed in the Putnamian manner in terms of which it is possible to assert all that is asserted by the *elucidandum*. In this case, however, the *elucidans* does not assert only what is asserted by the *elucidandum*, since it will have implications deriving from the theoretical apparatus in which it is embedded which the *elucidandum* does not have. The *elucidans*, in so far as it is correct, expresses everything that the *elucidandum* expresses, but not vice versa. The meaning relation between them is asymmetrical.

If I am right in this interpretation of Putnam's enterprise, we have here another remarkable parallel between Putnam's theory and the psycho-physical identity thesis. It is sometimes argued in objecting to the psycho-physical identity view that if something A is identical with something else B, anything that is predicable of A must be predicable of B and vice versa. It is then objected[10] that sensations cannot be identical with brain processes, since there are things which can be predicated of sensations that cannot be predicated of brain processes, and things that can be predicated of brain processes that cannot be predicated of sensations. Now it is not difficult to show that there are things predicable of brain processes—the number and location of the neurons, the nature of the physico-chemical processes involved, etc.—which are not predicable of mental processes. It is much more difficult to show that sensations have properties that brain processes could not have. I have argued[11] that there is no case for ascribing properties to sensations which brain processes could not have, provided we remember that the properties we are talking about are the properties of the process of having or experiencing a given sensation, rather than the properties of the sensations themselves treated as if they could somehow exist independently of someone's experiencing or having them; and I have yet to see a convincing refutation of this contention.[12] To show that there are properties predicable of having sensations which cannot in principle be predicated of brain processes would undoubtedly constitute a decisive refutation of

[10] See for example James W. Cornman, "The Identity of Mind and Body," *Journal of Philosophy*, LIX, 1962, pp. 486-492.

[11] "Is Consciousness a Brain Process?," pp. 49-50 in the original article and pp. 108-109 in Chappell, *op. cit.*

[12] The most difficult objection to meet is that of Kurt Baier ("Smart on Sensations," *Australasian Journal of Philosophy*, XL, 1962, pp. 57-68), who argues that privacy is a property of mental processes that brain processes in principle cannot have. Baier's objection is best met, I suggest, by pointing out that the privacy of mental processes is not a property. It is merely the absence of a property (public observability) which is in some sense predicable of brain processes. Of the adjectives listed by Cornman, *op. cit.*, p. 490 only 'intense,' 'unbearable,' and 'fading' are predicable of the experience itself. I find no difficulty in predicating these of brain processes.

E

the thesis in the form in which I hold it, since the hypothesis that the experiencing of *this* sensation is *that* brain process could only be verified by showing that the relevant brain process has all the properties that the mental process has. It is not, however, an objection to the thesis in the form in which I held that the brain processes have, as they clearly do have, properties that the mental process does not have.

What many people who discuss the psycho-physical identity thesis seem to overlook is that the identity relation that is being asserted between brain processes and mental processes is not a symmetrical relationship of equivalence. The thesis is that mental processes are brain processes and nothing else, but not the thesis that certain brain processes are mental processes and nothing else. Clearly any brain process that might be identified as being a given mental process would have many other properties besides being that mental process, just as an electric discharge through the atmosphere has many other properties besides being lightning. We do not want to say that an electric discharge through the atmosphere is lightning and nothing else; nor do we want to say that the old packing case is his table and nothing else, although we do or might want to say the converse. For this reason it is somewhat misleading to talk about the putative relationship between mental process and brain processes as a relationship of identity, particularly when addressing oneself to those who are accustomed to the notion of identity used in formal logic. In my original paper on this subject I referred to the "is" that relates lightning to electric discharge and which I wanted to say could sensibly be said to relate consciousness and brain processes as an "is" of composition rather than as an "is" of identity;[13] and this still seems to me a much better way of stating the thesis.[14]

[13] "Is Consciousness a Brain Process?," pp. 45-46 in the original article and pp. 102-103 in Chappell, *op. cit.*

[14] Professor J. J. C. Smart (personal communication) argues that once an identification of this kind becomes a matter of established scientific fact it becomes possible to apply to the original ordinary discourse concept all the predicates which are applicable to the scientific concept with which it has been identified, and that therefore the relationship is a genuine symmetrical identity and not, as I have argued, an asymmetrical relationship in which the predicates applicable to the ordinary discourse concept apply to the scientific concept, but not *vice versa*. Consideration of cases such as "lightning is an electric discharge through the atmosphere," "temperature is the amplitude of atomic motion," and "water is H_2O" suggests that Smart is right in his contention that once the identification becomes a matter of established scientific fact, there are no predicates predicable of the scientific concept which a scientist, at least, would be unwilling to apply to the ordinary discourse concept. I would maintain, however, that when and in so far as this state of affairs is reached, the ordinary discourse concept has undergone a definite change of meaning in the direction of assimilation to the scientific

To stress the asymmetry of the identity that is being asserted here is also to my mind a much better way than the method Putnam adopts of meeting the objection that to assert identity between pains and brain processes, or between pains and the functional states of a probabilistic automaton involves a change in the ordinary meaning of the word 'pain.' Putnam tries to dodge this objection, to which his theory is as much exposed as is the psycho-physical identity theory, by saying that we have no precise criteria for a change of meaning here. I am unhappy about this solution. For to say we have no precise criteria for deciding when a "change of meaning" or "an extension of usage" has occurred would appear to suggest that we have no means of deciding such issues, and hence that the very substantial part of linguistics and philosophy that is based on the assumption that such decisions can be reached is a complete waste of time. Now it may well be true that we do not have any precise criteria, which can be stated at the present time, for deciding whether or not we are using a word in the same or in different senses from one occasion to another. But it does not follow from this that we have no way of deciding such issues. People do not usually need to consult a rule book or a lexicon to decide whether a word or expression means the same thing in one context as it does in another. Nor do they have to learn any rules by heart to be able to do so. It may be helpful for certain theoretical purposes to talk as if people apply rules and criteria when they decide issues of this kind; but if so, it is important to remember that these rules and criteria are rules and criteria of a rather peculiar kind, which people can apply perfectly well without being able to state the rules and criteria they are applying. We can only state what the rules and criteria are by studying the way they are applied. The ability to make the relevant distinctions is logically prior to and presupposed by any attempt to state the criteria involved and hence no consequences about the possibility or impossibility of deciding such

---

concept with which it has been identified and that the identity relation has, by virtue of this process of assimilation, ceased to be a *synthetic* relation and become *analytic*. A liquid which had the appearance and all the commonly recognised properties of water would not now be called "water" by the chemist if its chemical formula was not H_2O. It would no longer be an exception to what was once an empirical hypothesis to the effect that what the layman calls "water" is always a substance with the chemical formula H_2O. I would contend that so long as the identity remains a matter of empirical hypothesis the relationship is asymmetrical in the sense that the predicates applying to the scientific concept can only be applied to the ordinary discourse concept on the assumption that the hypothesis is correct. To anyone who questions the hypothesis, they remain logically inapplicable or at least of doubtful application in the way that it must at one time have appeared logically inappropriate to apply the concept of "wave-length" to the ordinary concept "light."

issues follow from the fact that we cannot state criteria we apply in deciding them.

I should prefer to defend Putnam's theory, and my own in so far as it involves his, by saying that it is not an objection to a functional characterization of pain in terms of a machine model that this characterization involves (as we can surely agree it does) a change in the meaning of 'pain' in the sense of introducing new conceptual elements which are not implied by the current use of the term. This is not an objection to his thesis, because he is offering an elucidation of the concept of pain in terms of a machine model, not a translation. It is, however, an objection to such a characterization that it involves a change of meaning in the sense of failing to include some feature which is built into our current concept of pain. This must be evidence against any theory of what pain is, since "pain" is an ordinary discourse concept and hence any account of what we mean by 'pain' which is inconsistent with the way the term is ordinarily used is not an account of 'pain' as we ordinarily use the word.

MUSIC DISCOMPOSED

STANLEY CAVELL

I

It is a widespread opinion that aesthetics, as we think of it, became
a subject, and acquired its name, just over two hundred years ago;
which would make it the youngest of the principal branches of
philosophy. Nothing further seems to be agreed about it, not even
whether it is one subject, nor if so, what it should include, nor
whether it has the right name, nor what the name should be taken
to mean, nor whether given its problems, philosophers are particularly suited to venture them. Various reasons for these doubts
suggest themselves: (1) The problems of composers, painters,
poets, novelists, sculptors, architects . . . are internal to the procedures of each, and nothing general enough to apply to all could
be of interest to any. One cannot, I think, or ought not, miss the
truth of that claim, even while one feels that its truth needs correct
placement. There *are* people recognizable as artists, and all produce
works which we acknowledge, in some sense, to call for and warrant
certain kinds of experience. (2) There is an established activity and a
recognizable class of persons whose established task it is to discuss
the arts, namely the criticism and the critics of literature, painting,
music. . . . This fact faces two ways: One way, it suggests that there
is something importantly common to the arts, namely, that they all
require, or tolerate, such an activity; and that itself may incite
philosophical reflection. Another way, it suggests that only someone
competent as a critic of art is competent to speak of art at all, at least
from the point of view of the experience which goes into it or
which is to be found in it, so that an aesthetician incapable of
producing criticism is simply incapable of recognizing and relevantly describing the objects of his discourse. (3) It is not clear
what the data of the subject shall be. The enterprise of epistemolo-
gists, however paradoxical its conclusions have been, begins and
continues with examples and procedures common to all men; and
moral philosophers of every taste agree in appealing to the experience, the concepts, and the conflicts all men share. But upon
what, or whom, does the aesthetician focus? On the artist? On the
work he produces? On what the artist says about his work? On
what critics say about it? On the audience it acquires?

One familiar resolution of these questions has been to commend

the artist's remarks, and his audience's responses, to the attention
of psychologists or sociologists, confining philosophy's attention to
"the object itself." The plausibility of this resolution has strong
sources. There is the distinction established in the philosophy of
science according to which the philosopher's concern is confined to
the "context of justification" of a theory, its "context of discovery"
yielding, at best, to history and psychology. There is the decisive
accomplishment, in literary criticism, of the New Critics, whose
formalist program called for, and depended upon, minute attention
concentrated on the poem itself. There is, finally, the realization
on the part of anyone who knows what art is that many of the
responses directed to works of art are irrelevant to them as art and
that the artist's intention is *always* irrelevant—it no more counts
toward the success or failure of a work of art that the artist intended
something other than is *there*, than it counts, when the referee is
counting over a boxer, that the boxer had intended to duck.

I cannot accept such a resolution, for three main sorts of reasons:
(1) The fact that the criticism of art may, and even must, be formal
(in the sense suggested) implies nothing whatever about what the
content of aesthetics may or must be. Kant's aesthetics is, I take it,
supposed to be formal, but that does not deter Kant from introducing
intention (anyway, "purposiveness") and a certain kind of response
("disinterested pleasure") in determining the grounds on which
anything is to count as art. And such books as *The Birth of Tragedy*
and *What Is Art?* rely fundamentally on characterizing the experience of the artist and of his audience, and I am more sure that
Nietzsche (for all his reputedly unsound philology) and Tolstoy
(for all his late craziness) know what art is than I know what
philosophy or psychology are, or ought to be. (2) The denial of the
relevance of the artist's intention is likely not to record the simple,
fundamental fact that what an artist meant cannot alter what he
has or has not accomplished, but to imply a philosophical *theory*
according to which the artist's intention is something in his mind
while the work of art is something out of his mind, and so the closest
connection there could be between them is one of causation, about
which, to be sure, only a psychologist or biographer could care. But
I am far less sure that any such philosophical theory is correct than
I am that when I experience a work of art I feel that I am *meant* to
notice one thing and not another, that the placement of a note or
rhyme or line has a *purpose*, and that certain works are perfectly
realized, or contrived, or meretricious . . . . (3) Nothing could be
commoner among critics of art than to ask *why* the thing is as it is,
and characteristically to put this question, for example, in the
form "Why does Shakespeare follow the murder of Duncan with a
scene which begins with the sound of knocking?," or "Why does

Beethoven put in a bar of rest in the last line of the fourth Bagatelle
(Op. 126)?" The best critic is the one who knows best where to ask
this question, and how to get an answer; but surely he doesn't feel
it necessary, or desirable even were it possible, to get in touch
with the artist to find out the answer. The philosopher may,
because of his theory, explain that such questions are misleadingly
phrased, and that they really refer to the object itself, not to Shakespeare or Beethoven. But who is misled, and about what? An
alternative procedure, and I think sounder, would be to accept the
critic's question as perfectly appropriate—as, so to speak, a philosophical datum—and then to look for a philosophical explanation
which can accommodate that fact. Of course, not just *any* critic's
response can be so taken. And this suggests a further methodological
principle in philosophizing about art. It seems obvious enough that
in setting out to speak about the arts one begins with a rough
canon of the objects to be spoken about. It seems to me equally
necessary, in appealing to the criticism of art for philosophical
data, that one begin with a rough canon of criticism which is not
then repudiated in the philosophy to follow.

Confusion prescribes caution, even if the confusion is private and
of one's own making. Accordingly, I restrict my discussion here
primarily to one art, music; and within that art primarily to one
period, since the second World War; and within that period to
some characteristic remarks made by theorists of music about the
avant garde composers who regard themselves as the natural successors to the work of Schoenberg's greatest pupil, Anton Webern.
Though narrow in resource, however, my motives will seem
extremely pretentious, because I am going to raise a number of
large questions about art and philosophy and ways they bear on one
another. Let me therefore say plainly that I do not suppose myself
to have *shown* anything at all; that what I set down I mean merely
as suggestions; and that I am often not sure that they are
philosophically relevant. They are the result, at best, of a clash
between what I felt missing in the philosophical procedures I have
some confidence in, and what I feel present and significant in some
recent art.

II

I believe it is true to say that modernist art—roughly, the art
of one's own generation—has not become a problem for the philosophy contemporary with it (in England and America anyway);
and perhaps that is typical of the aesthetics of any period. I do
not wish to insist upon a particular significance in that fact, but I am
inclined to believe that there is decisive significance in it. For
example, it mars the picture according to which aesthetics stands to

art or to criticism as the philosophy of, say, physics stands to physics; for no one, I take it, could claim competence at the philosophy of physics who was not immediately concerned with the physics current in his time. One may reply that this is merely a function of the differences between science and art—the one progressing, outmoding, or summarizing its past, the other not. I would not find that reply very satisfactory, for two related reasons: (1) It obscures more than it reveals. It is not clear what it is about science which allows it to "progress" or, put another way, what it is which is called "progress" in science (for example, it does not progress evenly);[1] moreover, the succession of styles of art, though doubtless it will not simply constitute progress, nevertheless seems not to be mere succession either. Art critics and historians (not to mention artists) will often say that the art of one generation has "solved a problem" inherited from its parent generation; and it seems right to say that there is progress during *certain* stretches of art and with respect to certain developments within them (say the developments leading up to the establishment of sonata form, or to the control of perspective, or to the novel of the nineteenth century). Moreover, the succession of art styles is *irreversible*, which may be as important a component of the concept of progress as the component of superiority. And a new style not merely replaces an older one, it may change the significance of any earlier style; I do not think this is merely a matter of changing taste but a matter also of changing the *look*, as it were, of past art, changing the ways it can be described, outmoding some, bringing some to new light—one may even want to say, it can change what the past *is*, however against the grain that sounds. A generation or so ago, "Debussy" referred to music of a certain ethereal mood, satisfying a taste for refined sweetness or poignance; today it refers to solutions for avoiding tonality: I find I waver between thinking of that as a word altering its meaning and thinking of it as referring to an altered object. (2) Critics, on whom the philosopher may rely for his data, *are* typically concerned with the art of their time, and what they find it relevant to say about the art of any period will be moulded by that concern. If I do not share those concerns, do I understand what the critic means? Virtually every writer I have read on the subject of non-tonal music will at some point, whether he likes it or not, compare this music explicitly with tonal music; a critic like Georg Lukacs will begin a book by comparing (unfavorably) Bourgeois Modernism with the Bourgeois Realism of the nineteenth century; Clement Greenberg will write, "From Giotto to Courbet, the painter's first task had been to hollow out an illusion of three-dimensional space on a flat surface . . . . This spatial illusion

[1] See Thomas Kuhn, *The Structure of Scientific Revolutions*, Chicago, 1962.

or rather the sense of it, is what we may miss [in Modernism] even more than we do the images that used to fill it." Now, do I understand these comparisons if I do not share their experience of the modern? I do not mean merely that I shall not then understand what they say about modern art; I mean that I shall not then understand what they see in traditional art: I feel I am *missing* something about art altogether, something, moreover, which an earlier critic could not give me.

III

The writing I have begun studying, and upon which I base my observations, occurs largely in two sets of professional periodicals: *Die Reihe*, whose first issue appeared in 1955; and *Perspectives of New Music*, starting in 1962.[2] Both were created in direct response to "the general problems relating to the composition of music in our time," as the prefatory note to *Die Reihe's* first number puts it. Opening these periodicals, and allowing time to adapt to the cross-glare of new terms, symbols invented for the occasion, graphs, charts, some equations . . . several general characteristics begin to emerge as fairly common to their contents. There is, first, an obsession with *new-ness* itself, every other article taking some position about whether the novelty of the new music is radical, or less than it seems, whether it is aberrant or irreversible, whether it is the end of music as an art, or a reconception which will bring it new life. None, that I recall, raises the issue as a problem to be investigated, but as the cause of hope or despair or fury or elation. It is characteristic to find, in one and the same article, analyses of the most intimidating technicality and arcane apparatus, combined or ended with a mild or protracted cough of philosophy (e.g., "The new music aspires to Being, not to Becoming.)" If criticism has as its impulse and excuse the opening of access between the artist and his audience, giving voice to the legitimate claims of both, then there is small criticism in these pages—although there is a continuous reference to the *fact* that artist and audience are out of touch, and a frequent willingness to assign blame to one or the other of them. One is reminded that while the history of literary criticism is a part of the history of literature, and while the history of visual art is written by theorists and connoisseurs of art for whom an effort at accurate phenomenology can be as natural as the deciphering of iconography, histories of music contain virtually no criticism or assessment of their objects, but concentrate on details of its notation or its instruments or the occasions of its performance. The

---

[2] *Die Reihe*, Theodore Presser Co., Bryn Mawr, Pennsylvania, in association with Universal Edition. *Perspectives of New Music*, Princeton University Press.

serious attempt to articulate a *response* to a piece of music, where more than reverie, has characteristically stimulated mathematics or metaphysics—as though music has never quite become one of the facts of life, but shunts between an overwhelming directness and an overweening mystery. Is this because music, as we know it, is the newest of the great arts and just has not had the time to learn how to criticize itself; or because it inherently resists verbal transcriptions? (Both have been said, as both are said in accounting for the lack of a canon of criticism about the cinema.) Whatever the cause, the absence of humane music criticism (of course there are isolated instances) seems particularly striking against the fact that music has, among the arts, the most, perhaps the only, systematic and precise vocabulary for the description and analysis of its objects. Somehow that possession must itself be a liability; as though one now undertook to criticize a poem or novel armed with complete control of medieval rhetoric but ignorant of the modes of criticism developed in the past two centuries.

A final general fact about the writing in these periodicals is its concentration on the composer and his problems; a great many of the articles are produced by composers themselves, sometimes directly about, sometimes indirectly, their own music. Professor Paul Oskar Kristeller, in his review of the writing about the arts produced from Plato to Kant, notices in his final reflections that such writing has typically proceeded, and its categories and style thereby formed, from the spectator's or amateur's point of view.[3] Does the presence of these new journals of music indicate that the artist is, some place, finally getting the attention he deserves? But one can scarcely imagine a serious journal contributed to by major poets, novelists, or painters devoted to the problems of the making of poems and novels and paintings, nor that any such artist would find it useful if somehow it appeared. It might even be regarded by them as unseemly to wash these problems in public, and at best it distracts from the job of getting on with real work. Magazines are for interviews or for publishing one's work and having others write about it. Why is it not regarded as unseemly or distracting by composers? Perhaps it is. Then what necessity overrides a more usual artistic reticence? Perhaps it is an awareness that the problems composers face now are no longer merely private but are the problems of their art in general, "the general problems relating to the composition of music in our time." (This is likely to seem at once unmentionably obvious to composers and unintelligible to spectators, which is itself perhaps a measure of the problems of composition in our time.) This further suggests, as in the case of ordinary

[3] "The Modern System of the Arts," reprinted in *Renaissance Thought II*, New York, 1965, p. 225.

learned journals, the emergence of a new universal style or mode of procedure, implying an unparalleled dispersal of those who must inescapably be affected by one another's work. Painting still grows, as it always has, in particular cities; apprenticeship and imitation are still parts of its daily life. Writers do not share the severe burden of modernism which serious musicians and painters and sculptors have recognized for generations: a writer can still work with the words we all share, more or less, and have to share; he still, therefore, has an audience with the chance of responding to the way *he* can share the words more than more or less. My impression is that serious composers have, and feel they have, all but lost their audience, and that the essential reason for this (apart, for example, from the economics and politics of getting performances) has to do with crises in the internal, and apparently irreversible, developments within their own artistic procedures. This is what I meant by "the burden of modernism": the procedures and problems it now seems necessary to composers to employ and confront to make a work of art at all *themselves* insure that their work will not be comprehensible to an audience.

This comes closer to registering the dissonant and unresolved emotion in the pages to which I refer. They are prompted by efforts to communicate with an audience lost, and to compose an artistic community in disarray—efforts which only the art itself can accomplish. So the very existence of such periodicals suggests that they cannot succeed.

But here a difference of animus in these two periodicals becomes essential. *Die Reihe* began first, with an issue on electronic music, and its general tone is one of self-congratulation and eagerness for the future, whether it contains art and composers and performers or not. *Perspectives* began publication seven years later (and lean years or fat, seven years in our period may contain an artistic generation); and for a variety of reasons its tone is different. It is committed to much of the same music, shares some of the same writers, but the American publication is quite old world in its frequent concern with tradition and the artist and the performer and in its absence of belief that progress is assured by having *more* sounds and rhythms, etc., available for exploitation. Whatever the exact pattern of rancors and rites in these pages, the sense of conflict is unmistakable, and the air is of men fighting for their artistic lives. Perhaps, then, their theories and analyses are not addressed to an audience of spectators, but as has been suggested about their music itself, to one another. The communications often include artistic manifestos, with declarations of freedom and promises for the future. But unlike other manifestos, they are not meant to be personal; they do not take a position against an establishment, for they represent the establishment; a young composer, therefore, seems confronted not by one or another group of artists but by one or another official philosophy, and his artistic future may therefore seem to depend not on finding his own conviction but on choosing the right doctrine. Sometimes they sound like the dispassionate analyses and reports assembled in professional scientific and academic journals. But unlike those journals they are not organs of professional societies with fairly clear requirements for membership and universally shared criteria for establishing competence, even eminence, within them. One comes to realize that these professionals themselves do not quite know who is and who is not rightly included among their peers, whose work counts and whose does not. No wonder then, that we outsiders do not know. And one result clearly communicated by these periodicals is that there is no obvious way to find out.

What they suggest is that the possibility of fraudulence, and the experience of fraudulence, is endemic in the experience of contemporary music; that its full impact, even its immediate relevance, depends upon a willingness to trust the object, knowing that the time spent with its difficulties may be betrayed. I do not see how anyone who has experienced modern art can have avoided such experiences, and not just in the case of music. Is Pop Art art? Are canvases with a few stripes or chevrons on them art? Are the novels of Raymond Roussel or Robbe-Grillet? Are art movies? A familiar answer is that time will tell. But my question is: *What* will time tell? That certain departures in art-like pursuits have become established (among certain audiences, in textbooks, on walls, in college courses); that *someone* is treating them with the respect due, we feel, to art; that one no longer has the right to question their status? But in waiting for time to tell that, we miss what the present tells—that the dangers of fraudulence, and of trust, are essential to the experience of art. If anything in this paper should count as a thesis, that is my thesis. And it is meant quite generally. Contemporary music is only the clearest case of something common to modernism as a whole, and modernism only makes explicit and bare what has always been true of art. (That is almost a definition of modernism, not to say its purpose.) Aesthetics has so far been the aesthetics of the classics, which is as if we investigated the problem of other minds by using as examples our experience of *great* men or *dead* men. In emphasizing the experiences of fraudulence and trust as essential to the experience of art, I am in effect claiming that the answer to the question "What is art?" will in part be an answer which explains why it is we treat certain objects, or how we *can* treat certain objects, in ways normally reserved for treating persons.

Both Tolstoy's *What Is Art?* and Nietzsche's *Birth of Tragedy* begin from an experience of the fraudulence of the art of their time.

However obscure Nietzsche's invocation of Apollo and Dionysus and however simplistic Tolstoy's appeal to the artist's sincerity and the audience's "infection," their use of these concepts is to specify the genuine in art in opposition to specific modes of fraudulence, and their meaning is a function of that opposition. Moreover, they agree closely on what those modes of fraudulence are: in particular, a debased Naturalism's heaping up of random realistic detail, and a debased Romanticism's substitution of the stimulation and exacerbation of feeling in place of its artistic control and release; and in both, the constant search for "effects."

IV

How can fraudulent art be exposed? Not, as in the case of a forgery or counterfeit, by comparing it with the genuine article, for there *is* no genuine article of the right kind. Perhaps it helps to say: If we call it a matter of comparing something with the genuine article, we have to add (a) that what counts as the genuine article is not *given*, but itself requires critical determination; and (b) that what needs to be exposed is not that a work is a *copy*. (That of course *may* be an issue, and that *may* be an issue of forgery. Showing fraudulence is more like showing something is imitation—not: *an* imitation. The emphasis is not on copying a *particular* object, as in forgery and counterfeit, but on producing *the effect* of the genuine, or having some of its properties.) Again, unlike the cases of forgery and counterfeit, there is no one feature, or definite set of features, which may be described in technical handbooks, and no specific tests by which its fraudulence can be detected and exposed. Other frauds and imposters, like forgers and counterfeiters, admit *clear* outcomes, conclude in dramatic discoveries—the imposter is unmasked at the ball, you find the counterfeiters working over their press, the forger is caught signing another man's name, or he confesses. There are no such proofs possible for the assertion that the art accepted by a public is fraudulent; the artist himself may not know; and the critic may be shown up, not merely as incompetent, nor unjust in accusing the wrong man, but as taking others in (or out); that is, as an imposter.

The only exposure of false art lies in recognizing something about the object itself, but something whose recognition requires exactly the same capacity as recognizing the genuine article. It is a capacity not insured by understanding the language in which it is composed, and yet we may not understand what is said; nor insured by the healthy functioning of the senses, though we may be told we do not *see* or that we fail to *hear* something; nor insured by the aptness of our logical powers, though what we may have missed was the object's consistency or the way one thing followed from another. We may have missed its tone, or neglected an allusion or a cross current, or failed to see its point altogether; or the object may not have established its tone, or buried the allusion too far, or be confused in its point. You often do not know which is on trial, the object or the viewer: modern art did not invent this dilemma, it merely insists upon it. The critic will have to *get* us to see, or hear or realize or notice; help us to appreciate the tone; convey the current; point to a connection; show how to take the thing in. . . . What this getting, helping, conveying, and pointing consist in will be shown in the specific ways the critic accomplishes them, or fails to accomplish them. Sometimes you can say he is exposing an object to us (in its fraudulence, or genuineness); sometimes you can say he is exposing us to the object. (The latter is, one should add, not always a matter of noticing fine differences by exercising taste; sometimes it is a matter of admitting the lowest common emotion.) Accordingly, the critic's anger is sometimes directed at an object, sometimes at its audience, often at both. But sometimes, one supposes, it is produced by the frustrations inherent in his profession. He is part detective, part lawyer, part judge, in a country in which crimes and deeds of glory look alike, and in which the public not only, therefore, confuses one with the other, but does not know that one or the other has been committed; not because the news has not got out, but because what counts as the one or the other cannot be defined until it happens; and when it has happened there is no sure way he can get the news out; and no way at all without risking something like a glory or a crime of his own.

One line of investigation here would be to ask: Why does the assertion "You have to *hear* it!" mean what it does? Why is its sense conveyed with a word which emphasizes the function of a sense organ, and in the form of an imperative? The combination is itself striking. One cannot be commanded to hear a sound, though one can be commanded to listen to it, or for it. Perhaps the question is: How does it happen that the *achievement* or *result* of using a sense organ comes to be thought of as the *activity* of that organ—as though the aesthetic experience had the form not merely of a continuous effort (e.g., listening) but of a continuous achievement (e.g., hearing).

Why—on pain of what—must I hear it; what consequence befalls me if I don't? One answer might be: Well, then I wouldn't hear it—which at least says that there is no point to the hearing beyond itself; it is worth doing in itself. Another answer might be: Then I wouldn't *know* it (what it is about, what it is, what's happening, what is *there*). And what that seems to say is that works of art are objects of the sort that can only be *known in sensing*. It is not, as in the case of ordinary material objects, that I know *because* I see, or that seeing is *how* I know (as opposed, for example, to being told, or figuring it out). It is rather, one may wish to say, that *what* I know is what I see; or even: seeing *feels* like knowing. ('Seeing the point' conveys this sense, but in ordinary cases of seeing the point, once it's seen it's known, or understood; about works of art one may wish to say that they require a continuous seeing of the point.) Or one may even say: In such cases, knowing functions like an organ of sense. (The religious, or mystical, resonance of this phrase, while not deliberate, is welcome. For religious experience is subject to distrust on the same grounds as aesthetic experience is: by those to whom it is foreign, on the ground that its claims must be false; by those to whom it is familiar, on the ground that its quality must be tested.)

Another way one might try to capture the idea is by saying: Such objects are only *known by feeling*, or *in* feeling. This is not the same as saying that the object expresses feeling, or that the aesthetic response consists in a feeling of some sort. Those are, or may be, bits of a theory about the aesthetic experience and its object; whereas what I am trying to describe, or the descriptions I am trying to hit on, would at best serve as data for a theory. What the expression 'known by feeling' suggests are facts (or experiences) such as these: (1) What I know, when I've *seen* or *heard* something is, one may wish to say, not a matter of *merely* knowing it. But what more is it? Well, as the words say, it is a matter of *seeing* it. But one could also say that it is not a matter of *merely* seeing it. But what more is it? Perhaps "merely knowing" should be compared with "not really knowing": "You don't really know what it's like to be a Negro"; "You don't really know how your remark made her feel"; "You don't really know what I mean when I say that Schnabel's slow movements give the impression not of slowness but of infinite length." You merely say the words. The issue in each case is: What would *express* this knowledge? It is not that my knowledge will be real, or more than *mere* knowledge, when I acquire a particular feeling, or come to see something. For the issue can also be said to be: What would express the acquisition of that feeling, or show that you have seen the thing? And the answer might be that I now *know* something I didn't know before. (2) "Knowing by feeling" is not like "knowing by touching"; that is, it is not a case of providing the *basis* for a claim to know. But one could say that feeling functions as a touchstone: the mark left on the stone is out of the sight of others, but the result is one of knowledge, or has the form of knowledge—it is directed to an object, the object has been tested, the result is one of conviction. This seems to me to suggest why one is anxious to communicate the experience of such objects. It is not merely that I want to tell you how it is with me, how I feel, in order to find sympathy or to be left alone, or for any other of the reasons for which one reveals one's feelings. It's rather that I want to tell you something I've seen, or heard, or realized, or come to understand, for the reasons for which *such* things are communicated (because it is news, about a world we share, or could). Only I find that I can't *tell* you; and that makes it all the more urgent to tell you. I want to tell you because the knowledge, unshared, is a burden—not, perhaps, the way having a secret can be a burden, or being misunderstood; a little more like the way, perhaps, not being believed is a burden, or not being trusted. It matters that others know what I see, in a way it does not matter whether they know my tastes. It matters, there is a burden, because unless I can tell what I know, there is a suggestion (and to myself as well) that I do *not* know. But I *do*—what I see is *that* (pointing to the object). But for that to communicate, you have to see it too. Describing one's experience of art is itself a form of art; the burden of describing it is like the burden of producing it. Art is often praised because it brings men together. But it also separates them.

The list of figures whose art Tolstoy dismisses as fraudulent or irrelevant or bad, is, of course, unacceptably crazy: most of Beethoven, all of Brahms and Wagner; Michelangelo, Renoir; the Greek dramatists, Dante, Shakespeare, Milton, Goethe, Ibsen, Tolstoy . . . . But the sanity of his procedure is this: it confronts the fact that we often do not find, and have never found, works we would include in a canon of works of art to be of importance or relevance to us. And the implication is that apart from this we cannot know that they are art, or what makes them art. One could say: objects so canonized do not exist for us. This strikes Tolstoy as crazy—as though we were to say we know that there are other minds because other people have told us there are.

V

But I was discussing some writing now current about the new music. Perhaps I can say more clearly why it leads, or has led me, to these various considerations by looking at three concepts which recur in it over and over—the concepts of composition, improvisation, and chance.[4]

[4] Most of the material in this, and in the following two sections was presented as part of a symposium called "Composition, Improvisation and Chance," held at a joint meeting of the American Musicological Society, the Society for Ethnomusicology, and the College Music Society, at the University of California, Berkeley, December 1960. The title of the symposium, as well as my participation in it, were both the work of its moderator, Joseph Kerman. I am grateful to him also for suggestions about the initial material I presented at Berkeley and about an earlier draft of the present paper.

The reason for their currency can be put, roughly, this way. The innovations of Schoenberg (and Bartok and Stravinsky) were necessitated by a crisis of composition growing out of the increasing chromaticism of the nineteenth century which finally overwhelmed efforts to organize music within the established assumptions of tonality. Schoenberg's solution was the development of the twelve-tone system which, in effect, sought to overcome this destructiveness of chromaticism by accepting it totally, searching for ways to organize a rigidly recurring total chromatic in its own terms. History aside, what is essential is that no assumption is any longer to be made about how compositional centers or junctures could be established—e.g., by establishing the "dominant" of a key—and the problem was one of discovering what, in such a situation, could be heard as serving the structural functions tonality used to provide. Schoenberg's twelve-tone "rows" and the operations upon them which constitute his system, were orderings and operations upon pitches (or, more exactly, upon the familiar twelve classes of pitches). About 1950, composers were led to consider that variables of musical material other than its pitches could also be subjected to serial ordering and its Schoenbergian transformations—variables of rhythm, duration, density, timbre, dynamics, and so on. But now, given initial series of pitches, rhythms, timbres, dynamics, etc., together with a plot of the transformations each is to undergo, and a piece is written or, rather, determined; it is, so it is said, totally organized. What remains is simply to translate the rules into the notes and values they determine and see what we've got. Whether what such procedures produce is music or not, they certainly produced philosophy. And it is characteristic of this philosophy to appeal to the concepts of composition, chance, and improvisation.

The motives or necessities for these concepts are not always the same. In the writing of John Cage, chance is explicitly meant to *replace* traditional notions of art and composition; the radical ceding of the composer's control of his material is seen to provide a profounder freedom and perception than mere art, for all its searches, had found. In the defense of "total organization," on the contrary, chance and improvisation are meant to *preserve* the concepts of art and composition for music; to explain how, although the composer exercises choice only over the initial conditions of his work, the determinism to which he then yields his power itself creates the spontaneity and surprise associated with the experience of art; and either (a) because it produces combinations which are unforseen, or (b) because it includes directions which leave the performer free to choose, i.e., to improvise. It is scarcely unusual for an awareness of determinism to stir philosophical speculation about the possibilities of freedom and choice and responsibility. But whereas the more usual motivation has been to preserve responsibility in the face of determinism, these new views wish to preserve choice by foregoing responsibility (for everything but the act of "choosing").

Let us listen to one such view, from Ernst Krenek, who was for years a faithful disciple of Schoenberg and who has emerged as an important spokesman for total organization.

> Generally and traditionally "inspiration" is held in great respect as the most distinguished source of the creative process in art. It should be remembered that inspiration by definition is closely related to chance, for it is the very thing that cannot be controlled, manufactured or premeditated in any way. It is what falls into the mind (according to the German term *Einfall*) unsolicited, unprepared, unrehearsed, coming from nowhere. This obviously answers the definition of chance as "the absence of any known reason why an event should turn out one way rather than another." Actually the composer has come to distrust his inspiration because it is not really as innocent as it was supposed to be, but rather conditioned by a tremendous body of recollection, tradition, training, and experience. In order to avoid the dictations of such ghosts, he prefers to set up an impersonal mechanism which will furnish, according to premeditated patterns, unpredictable situations . . . the creative act takes place in an area in which it has so far been entirely unsuspected, namely in setting up the serial statements . . . What happens afterwards is predetermined by the selection of the mechanism, but not premeditated except as an unconscious result of the predetermined operations. The unexpected happens by necessity. The surprise is built in. ("Extents and Limits of Serial Techniques," *Musical Quarterly*, XLVI, 1960, pp. 228-229.)

This is not serious, but it is meant; and it is symptomatic—the way it is symptomatic that early in Krenek's paper he suggests that the twelve-tone technique "appears to be a special, or limiting, case of serial music, similar to an interpretation of Newtonian mechanics as a limiting expression of the Special Theory of Relativity, which in turn has been explained as a limiting expression of that General Theory." (Note the scientific caution of "appears to be.") The vision of our entire body of recollection, tradition, training, and experience as so many ghosts *could* be serious. It was serious, in their various ways, for Kierkegaard, Marx, Nietzsche, Emerson, Ibsen, Freud, and for most of the major poets and novelists of the past hundred years. It is not merely a modern problem; it is, one could say, the problem of modernism, the attempt in every work to do what has never been done, because what is known is known to be insufficient, or worse. It is an old theme of tragedy that we will be responsible for our actions beyond anything we bargain for, and it is the prudence of morality to have provided us with excuses and virtues against that time. Krenek turns this theme into the comedy of making choices whose consequences we accept as the very embodiment of our will and sensibility although we cannot, in principle, see our responsibility in them. He says that "the composer has come to distrust his inspiration," but he obviously does not mean what those words convey—that the composer (like, say, Luther or Lincoln) is gripped by an idea which is causing him an agony of doubt. What in fact Krenek has come to distrust is the composer's capacity to feel any idea as his own. In denying tradition, Krenek is a Romantic, but with no respect or hope for the individual's resources; and in the reliance on rules, he is a Classicist, but with no respect or hope for his culture's inventory of conventions.

It is less my wish here to detail the failings or to trace the symptoms in such philosophizing as Krenek's, than it is to note simply that theorizing of this kind is characteristic of the writing about new music—alternating, as was suggested, with purely technical accounts of the procedures used in producing the work. For this fact in itself suggests (1) that such works cannot be *criticized*, as traditional art is criticized, but must be defended, or rejected, as art altogether; and (2) that such work would not exist but for the philosophy. That, in turn, suggests that the activity going into the production, or consumption, of such products cannot be satisfied by the art it yields, but only in a philosophy which seems to give justification and importance to the activity of producing it. I am not suggesting that such activity is in fact unimportant, nor that it can in no way be justified, but only that such philosophizing as Krenek's does not justify it and must not be used to protect it against aesthetic assessment. (Cage's theorizing, which I find often quite charming, is exempt from such strictures, because he clearly believes that the work it produces is no more important than the theory is, and that it is not justified by the theory, but, as it were, illustrates the theory. That his work is performed as music—rather than a kind of paratheatre or parareligious exercise—is only another sign of the confusions of the age. I do not speak of his music explicitly meant to accompany the dance.)

I have suggested that it is significant not only *that* philosophy should occur in these ways, but also that it should take the content it has. I want now to ask why it is that the concepts of chance and improvisation should occur at all in discussing composition; what might they be used to explain?

VI

What is composition, what is it to compose? It seems all right to say, "It is to make something, an object of a particular sort." The question then is, "What sort?" One direction of reply would be, "An object of art." And what we need to know is just what an object of art is. Suppose we give a minimal answer: "It is an object in which human beings will or can take an interest, one which will or can absorb or involve them." But we can be absorbed by lots of things people make: toys, puzzles, riddles, scandals . . . . Still, something is said, because not *everything* people make is an object of this sort. It is a problem, an artistic problem—an experimental problem, one could say—to discover what will have the capacity to absorb us the way art does. Could someone be interested and become absorbed in a pin, or a crumpled handkerchief? Suppose someone did. Shall we say, "It's a matter of taste"? We might dismiss him as mad (or suppose he is pretending), or, alternatively, ask ourselves what he can possibly be *seeing in* it. That these *are* our alternatives is what I wish to emphasize. The situation demands an explanation, the way watching someone listening intently to Mozart, or working a puzzle, or, for that matter, watching a game of baseball, does not. The forced choice between the two responses— "He's mad" (or pretending, or hypnotized, etc.) or else "What's in it?"—are the imperative choices we have when confronted with a new development in art. (A revolutionary development in science is different: not because the new move can initially be proved to be valid—perhaps it can't, in the way we suppose that happens—but because it is easier, for the professional community, to spot cranks and frauds in science than in art; and because if what the innovator does is valid, then it is *eo ipso* valid for the rest of the professional community, *in their own work*, and as it stands, as well.) But objects of art not merely interest and absorb, they move us; we are not merely involved with them, but concerned with them, and care about them; we treat them in special ways, invest them with a value which normal people otherwise reserve only for other people— *and* with the same kind of scorn and outrage. They *mean* something to us, not just the way statements do, but the way people do. People devote their lives, sometimes sacrifice them, to producing such objects just in order that they will have such consequences; and we do not think they are mad for doing so. We approach such objects not merely because they are interesting in themselves, but because they are felt as made by someone—and so we use such categories as intention, personal style, feeling, dishonesty, authority, inventiveness, profundity, metriciousness, etc., in speaking of them. The category of intention is as inescapable (or escapable with the

same consequences) in speaking of objects of art as in speaking of
what human beings say and do: without it, we would not understand
what they are. They are, in a word, not works of nature but of *art*
(i.e., of act, talent, skill). Only the concept of intention does not
function, as elsewhere, as a term of excuse or justification. We follow
the progress of a piece the way we follow what someone is saying or
doing. Not, however, to see how it will come out, nor to learn
something specific, but to see what *it* says, to see what someone has
been able to make out of these materials. A work of art does not
express some particular intention (as statements do), nor achieve
particular goals (the way technological skill and moral action do),
but, one may say, celebrates the fact that men can intend their lives
at all (if you like, that they are free to choose), and that their actions
are coherent and effective at all in the scene of indifferent nature and
determined society. This is what I understand Kant to have seen
when he said of works of art that they embody "purposiveness without purpose."

Such remarks are what occur to me in speaking of compositions
as objects *composed*. The concepts of chance and of improvision have
natural roles in such a view: the capacities for improvising and for
taking and seizing chances are virtues common to the activity leading
to a composition. It suggests itself, in fact, that these are two of the
virtues necessary to act coherently and successfully at all. I use
'virtue' in what I take to be Plato's and Aristotle's sense: a capacity
by virtue of which one is able to act successfully, to follow the
distance from an impulse and intention through to its realization.
Courage and Temperance are virtues because human actions move
precariously from desire and intention into the world, and one's
course of action will meet dangers or distractions which, apart from
courage and temperance, will thwart their realization. A world in
which you could get what you want merely by wishing would not
only contain no beggars, but no human activity. The success of an
action is threatened in other familiar ways: by the lack of preparation or foresight; by the failure of the most convenient resources,
natural or social, for implementing the action (a weapon, a bridge, a
shelter, an extra pair of hands); and by a lack of knowledge about
the best course to take, or way to proceed. To survive the former
threats will require ingenuity and resourcefulness, the capacity for
improvisation; to overcome the last will demand the willingness and
capacity to take and to seize chances.

Within the world of art one makes one's own dangers, takes one's
own chances—and one speaks of its objects at such moments in terms
of tension, problem, imbalance, necessity, shock, surprise . . . . And
within this world one takes and exploits these chances, finding,
through danger, an unsuspected security—and so one speaks of

fulfillment, calm, release, sublimity, vision . . . . Within it, also, the means of achieving one's purposes cannot lie at hand, ready-made. The means themselves have inevitably to be fashioned for *that* danger, and for *that* release—and so one speaks of inventiveness, resourcefulness, or else of imitativeness, obviousness, academicism. The *way* one escapes or succeeds is, in art, as important as the success itself; indeed, the way constitutes the success—and so the means that are fashioned are spoken of as masterful, elegant, subtle, profound. . . .

I said: in art, the chances you take are your own. But of course you are inviting others to take them with you. And since they are, nevertheless, your own, and your invitation is based not on power or authority, but on attraction and promise, your invitation incurs the most exacting of obligations: that *every* risk must be shown worthwhile, and every infliction of tension lead to a resolution, and every demand on attention and passion be satisfied—that risks those who trust you can't have known they would take, will be found to yield value they can't have known existed. The creation of art, being human conduct which affects others, has the commitments any conduct has. It escapes morality; not, however, in escaping commitment, but in being free to choose only those commitments it wishes to incur. In this way art plays with one of man's fates, the fate of being accountable for everything you do and are, intended or not. It frees us to sing and dance, gives us actions to perform whose consequences, commitments, and liabilities are discharged in the act itself. The price for freedom in this choice of commitment and accountability is that of an exactitude in meeting those commitments and discharging those accounts which no mere morality can impose. You cede the possibilities of excuse, explanation, or justification for your failures; and the cost of failure is not remorse and recompense, but the loss of coherence altogether.

The concept of improvisation, unlike the concept of chance, is one which has established and familiar uses in the practice of music theorists and historians. An ethnomusicologist will have recourse to the concept as a way of accounting for the creation-cum-performance of the music of cultures, or classes, which have no functionaries we would think of as composers, and no objects we would think of as embodying the intention to art; and within the realm of composed (written) music, improvision is, until recent times, recognized as explicitly called for at certain sharply marked incidents of a performance—in the awarding of cadenzas, in the opportunities of ornamentation, in the realization of figured bass. In such uses, the concept has little explanatory power, but seems merely to name events which one knows, as matters of historical fact (that is, as facts independent of anything a critic would have to discover by an analysis or interpretation of the musical material as an aesthetic phenomenon), not to have been composed.

My use of the concept is far more general. I mean it to refer to certain qualities of music generally. Perhaps what I am getting at can be brought out this way. In listening to a great deal of music, particularly to the time of Beethoven, it would, I want to suggest, be possible to imagine that it was being improvised. Its mere complexity, or a certain kind of complexity, would be no obstacle. (Bach, we are told, was capable of improvising double fugues on any given subjects.) I do not suggest that a chorus or a symphony orchestra can be imagined to be improvising its music; on the contrary, a group improvisation itself has a particular *sound*. On the other hand I do not wish to restrict the sense of improvisation to the performance of one player either. It may help to say: One can hear, in the music in question, how the composition is *related* to, or could grow in familiar ways, from a process of improvisation; as though the parts meted out by the composer were re-enactments, or dramatizations, of successes his improvisations had discovered— given the finish and permanence the occasion deserves and the public demands, but containing essentially only such discoveries. If this could be granted, a further suggestion becomes possible. Somewhere in the development of Beethoven, this ceases to be imaginable. (I do not include *all* music after Beethoven. Chopin and Lizst clearly seem improvisatory, in the sense intended; so do Brahms *Intermezzi*, but not Brahms *Symphonies*; early Stravinsky, perhaps, but not recent Stravinsky.)

Why might such a phenomenon occur? It is, obviously enough, within contexts fully defined by shared formulas that the possibility of full, explicit improvisation traditionally exists—whether one thinks of the great epics of literature (whose "oral-formulaic" character is established), or of ancient Chinese painting, or of Eastern music, or of the theatre of the Commedia dell'Arte, or jazz. If it seems a paradox that the reliance on formula should allow the fullest release of spontaneity, that must have less to do with the relation of these phenomena than with recent revolutions in our aesthetic requirements. The suggestion, however, is this. The context in which we can hear music as improvisatory is one in which the language it employs, its conventions, are familiar or obvious enough (whether because simple or because they permit of a total mastery or perspicuity) that at no point are we or the performer in doubt about our location or goal; there are solutions to every problem, permitting the exercise of familiar forms of resourcefulness; a mistake is clearly recognizable as such, and may even present a chance to be seized; and just as the general range of chances is circumscribed, so there is a preparation for every chance, and if not an inspired one, then a formula for one. But in the late experience of Beethoven, it is as if our freedom to act no longer depends on the possibility of spontaneity; improvising to fit a *given* lack or need is no longer enough. The entire enterprise of action and of communication has become problematic. The problem is no longer how to do what you want, but to know what would satisfy you. We could also say: Convention as a whole is now looked upon not as a firm inheritance from the past, but as a continuing improvisation in the face of problems we no longer understand. Nothing we now have to say, no *personal* utterance, has its meaning conveyed in the conventions and formulas we now share. In a time of slogans, sponsored messages, ideologies, psychological warfare, mass projects, where words have lost touch with their sources or objects, and in a phonographic culture where music is for dreaming, or for kissing, or for taking a shower, or for having your teeth drilled, our choices seem to be those of silence, or nihilism (the denial' of the value of shared meaning altogether), or statements so personal as to form the possibility of communication without the support of convention—perhaps to become the source of new convention. And then, of course, they are most likely to fail even to seem to communicate. Such, at any rate, are the choices which the modern works of art I know seem to me to have made. I should say that the attempt to re-invent convention is the alternative I take Schoenberg and Stravinsky and Bartok to have taken; whereas the total organization of Krenek (at present) and Stockhausen has chosen nihilism.

VII

The sketches I have given of possible roles of improvisation and chance in describing composition obviously do not fit their use in the ideology of the new music; they may, however, help understand what that ideology is. When a contemporary theorist appeals to *chance*, he obviously is not appealing to its associations with taking and seizing chances, with risks and opportunities. The point of the appeal is not to call attention to the act of composition, but to deny that act; to deny that what he offers is composed. His concept is singular, with no existing plural; it functions not as an explanation for particular actions but as a metaphysical principle which supervises his life and work as a whole. The invocation of chance is like an earlier artist's invocation of the muse, and serves the same purpose: to indicate that his work comes not from *him*, but *through* him—its validity or authority is not a function of his own powers or intentions. Speaking for the muse, however, was to give voice to what all men share, or all would hear; speaking through chance foregoes a voice altogether—there is nothing to say. (That is, of course, by now a cliché of popular modernism.) This way of foregoing composition may perhaps usefully be compared with the way it is foregone in modernist painting. The contemporary English sculptor Anthony Caro is reported to have said: "I do not compose." Whatever he meant by that, it seems to have clear relevance to the painting of abstract expressionism and what comes after.[5] If you look at a Pollock drip painting or at a canvas consisting of eight parallel stripes of paint, and what you are looking for is *composition* (matters of balance, form, reference among the parts, etc.), the result is absurdly trivial: a child could do it; I could do it. The question, therefore, if it is art, must be: How is this to be seen? What is the painter doing? The problem, one could say, is not one of escaping inspiration, but of determining how a man could be inspired to do *this*, why he feels *this* necessary or satisfactory, how he can *mean* this. Suppose you conclude that he cannot. Then that will mean, I am suggesting, that you conclude that this is not art, and this man is not an artist; that in failing to mean what he's done, he is fraudulent. But how do you know?

In remarking the junctures at which composers have traditionally called for improvisation (cadenzas, figured bass, etc.), I might have put that by saying that the composer is at these junctures leaving something open to the performer. It is obvious that throughout the first decades of this century composers became more and more explicit in their notations and directions, leaving less and less open to the performer. One reason for allowing improvisation in the new music has been described as returning *some* area of freedom to the performer in the midst of specifications so complex and frequent (each note may have a different tempo, dynamic marking, and direction for attack, at extreme rates of speed) that it is arguable they have become unrealizable in practice. Does this use of "something left open" suggest that we have an idea of some notation which may be "complete," closing all alternatives save one to the performer? And is the best case of "leaving nothing open" one in which the composer codes his music directly into his "performer," thus obviating any need for an intermediary between him and his

---

[5] Reported by Michael Fried (who showed me its significance) in an article on Caro in *The Lugano Review*, 1965. This is my first opportunity to acknowledge a pervasive indebtedness to Michael Fried, to whose guidance is due any understanding I have come to about modernist painting and sculpture. Conversations with him are implicit in many formulations and concerns both of this paper and of the replies which follow its commentators. See, for example, his *Three American Painters*, the catalogue essay for an exhibition of the work of Noland, Olitski, and Stella, at the Fogg Museum, in the spring of 1965; and his "Jules Olitski's New Paintings," *Artforum*, November 1965.

audience? What would be the significance of this displacement? A composer might be relieved that at least he would no longer have to suffer bad performances, and one might imagine a gain in having all performances uniform. But perhaps what would happen is that there would, for music made that way, no longer be anything we should call a "performance"; the concept would have no use there, anymore than it has for seeing movies. (One goes to see Garbo's performance as Camille, but not to see a performance of (the movie) *Camille*.) Perhaps, then, one would go to "soundings," "first plays," and "re-runs" of pieces of music. And then other musical institutions would radically change, e.g., those of apprenticeship, of conservatories, of what it is one studies and practices to become a composer. Would we then go on calling such people composers? But of course everything depends upon just what we are imagining his procedures to be. If, for example, he proceeds only so far as Krenek's "initial choices" and accepts whatever then results, I think we would not; but if, even if he begins that way, we believe that he has in some way tested the result on himself, with a view to satisfying himself—even if we do not know, or he does not know, what the source of satisfaction is—then perhaps we would. If we would not, would this suggest that the concept of a composition is essentially related to the concept of a performance? What it suggests is that it is not clear what is and is not essentially connected to the concept of music.

I do not, however, hesitate, having reminded myself of what the notion of improvisation suggests, to say that what is called for in a piece such as Stockhausen's *Pianostück Elf* (where nineteen fragments are to be selected from, in varying orders, depending upon certain decisions of the performer) is not improvisation. (The main reason, I think, for my withholding of the concept, is that nothing counts as the *goal* of a performance.) To call it improvisation is to substitute for the real satisfactions of improvisation a dream of spontaneity— to match the dream of organization it is meant to complement; as Krenek's fantasy of physics substitutes for the real satisfaction of knowledge. It also, since improvisation implies shared conventions, supposes that you can create a living community at a moment's notice. A similar point occurs when such a work is praised, as it has been, on the ground that it is graphically lovely. It is, I think, quite pretty to look at, but so is a Chopin or Bach or medieval manuscript graphically satisfying. To rest one's hope for organization on such an admittedly pleasant quality is to suppose that you can become a visual artist inadvertently. It expresses the same contempt for the artistic process as calling something musically organized (let alone totally organized) on grounds unrelated to any way in which it is, or is meant to be, heard.

VIII

Why, instead of philosophy, didn't music made in these ways produce laughter and hostility? It did, of course, and does. But the response couldn't end there, because nobody could *prove* it wasn't music. Of course not, because it is not clear that the notion of "proving it is (or is not) music" is even intelligible, which means that it is not fully intelligible to say that nobody could do what it describes. (*What* can't anybody do here?) My suggestion is only that some composers would have had the remarkable feeling that their lives depended on performing this indescribable task. Why? Because those productions themselves seemed to prove something, namely, that music (or whatever it is) produced in those ways was indistinguishable from, or close enough to music produced in traditional ways—by composers, that is, artists, from their inspiration and technique, both painfully acquired, and out of genuine need—to be confused with it, and therewith certain to replace it. (It's just as good, and so much easier to make.) And it seemed to prove that the detractors of modernism were right all along: whatever artists and aestheticians may have said about the internal and coherent development of the art, it all turns out to have arrived at pure mechanism, it has no *musical* significance, a child could do it. This, or something like it, had been said about Beethoven, about Stravinsky, and doubtless about every *avant garde* in the history of the arts. Only no child ever *did* it before, and *some* people obviously did find it musically significant. Saint-Saëns stormed out of the first performance of *The Rite of Spring*. But Ravel and serious young composers stayed and were convinced. But now a child *has* done it, or might as well have, and a child could understand it as well as anyone else—you prove he couldn't. It is, I take it, significant about modernism and its "permanent revolution" that its audience recurrently tells itself the famous stories of riots and walkouts and outrages that have marked its history. It is as though the *impulse* to shout fraud and storm out is always present, but fear of the possible consequence overmasters the impulse. Remember Saint-Saëns: He said the Emperor had no clothes, and then history stripped him naked. The philistine audience cannot afford to admit the new; the *avant garde* audience cannot afford not to. This bankruptcy means that both are at the mercy of their tastes, or fears, and that no artist can test his work either by their rejection or by their acceptance.

These may or may not exhaust all the audiences there are, but they certainly do not include all the people there are. This suggests that genuine responses to art are to be sought in individuals alone, as the choice or affinity for a canon of art and a canon of criticism must be made by individuals alone; and that these individuals have no audience to belong in as sanctioning, and as sharing the responsibility for, the partiality they show for the work of individual artists and particular critics. (As the faithful auditor of God is perhaps no longer to be expected, and cannot receive sanction, through membership in a congregation.) This suggests one way of putting the modern predicament of audience: taste now appears as partialness.

This is the point at which Nietzsche's perception outdistances Tolstoy's. Tolstoy called for sincerity from the artist and infection from his audience; he despised taste just because it revealed, and concealed, the loss of our *appetite* for life and consequently for art that matters. But he would not face the possible cost of the artist's radical, unconventionalized sincerity—that his work may become uninfectious, and even (and even deliberately) unappetizing, forced to defeat the commonality which was to be art's high function, in order to remain art at all (art in exactly the sense Tolstoy meant, directed from and to genuine need). Nietzsche became the unbalanced ledger of that cost, whereas Tolstoy apparently let himself imagine that we could simply *stop* our reliance on taste once we were told that it was blocking us to satisfaction—and not merely in art. What modern artists realize, rather, is that taste must be *defeated*, and indeed that this can be accomplished by nothing less powerful than art itself. One may see in this the essential moral motive of modern art. Or put it this way: What looks like "breaking with tradition" in the successions of art is not really that; or is that only after the fact, looking historically or critically; or is that only as a result not as a motive: the unheard of appearance of the modern in art is an effort not to break, but to keep faith with tradition. It is perhaps fully true of Pop Art that its motive is to break with the tradition of painting and sculpture; and the result is not that the tradition is broken, but that these works are irrelevant to that tradition, i.e., they are not paintings, whatever their pleasures. (Where history has cunning, it is sometimes ironic, but sometimes just.)

IX

I said earlier that the periodicals about music which we were discussing were trying to do what only the art of music itself could do. But maybe it just is a fact about modern art that coming to care about it demands coming to care about the problems in producing it. Whatever painting may be about, modernist painting is about *painting*, about what it means to use a limited two-dimensional surface in ways establishing the coherence and interest we demand of art. Whatever music can do, modern music is concerned with the making of music, with what is required to gain the movement and the stability on which its power depends. The problems of composition are no longer irrelevant to the audience of art when the solution to a compositional problem has become identical with the aesthetic result itself.

In this situation, criticism stands, or could, or should stand, in an altered relation to the art it serves. At any time it is subordinate to that art, and expendable once the experience of an art or period or departure is established. But in the modern situation it seems inevitable, even, one might say, internal, to the experience of art. One evidence of what I have in mind is the ease with which a new departure catches phrases which not merely free new response, but join in the creation of that response; moreover, the phrases do not cease to matter once the response is established, but seem required in order that the response be sustained. New theatre is "absurd"; new painting is "action"; Pop Art exists "between life and art"; in serial music "chance occurs by necessity." Often one does not know whether interest is elicited and sustained primarily by the object or by what can be said about the object. My suggestion is not that this is bad, but that it is definitive of a modernist situation. Perhaps it would be nicer if composers could not think, and felt no need to open their mouths except to sing—if, so to say, art did not present problems. But it does, and they do, and the consequent danger is that the words, because inescapable, will usurp motivation altogether, no longer tested by the results they enable. I think this has already happened in the phrases I cited a moment ago, and this suggests that a central importance of criticism has become to protect its art against criticism. Not just from bad criticism, but from the critical impulse altogether, which no longer knows its place, perhaps because it no longer has *a* place. In a Classical Age, criticism is confident enough to prescribe to its art without moralism and its consequent bad conscience. In a Romantic Age, art is exuberant enough to escape criticism without the loss of conscience—appealing, as it were, to its public directly. In a Modern Age, both that confidence and that appeal are gone, and are to be re-established, if at all, together, and in confusion.

If we say it is a gain to criticism, and to art, when we know that criticism must not be prescriptive (e.g., tell artists what they ought to produce), then we should also recognize that this injunction is *clear* only when we already accept an object as genuine art and a man as an authentic artist. But the modernist situation forces an awareness of the *difficulty* in avoiding prescription, and indeed of the ways in which criticism, and art itself, are ineluctably prescriptive— art, because its successes garner imitations, not just because there are always those who want success at any price, but because of the very authority which has gone into the success; criticism, not because the critic cannot avoid prescriptive utterances, but because the terms in which he defines his response themselves define which objects are and which are not relevant to his response. When, therefore, artists are unmoored from tradition, from taste, from audience, from their own past achievement; when, that is, they are brought to rely most intimately on the critic, if only the critic in themselves; then the terms in which they have learned to accept criticism will come to dictate the terms in which they will look for success: apart from these, nothing will count as successful because nothing will be evaluable, nothing have a chance of validity. Here the artist's survival depends upon his constantly eluding, and constantly assembling, his critical powers.

A certain use of mathematical-logical descriptions of tone-row occurrences is only the clearest case of these difficulties, as it is also the case which most clearly shows the force of the aesthetically and intellectually irrelevant in establishing a reigning criticism—in this case, the force of a fearful scientism, an intellectual chic which is at once intimidating and derivative, and in general the substitution of precision for accuracy. This is hardly unusual, and it should go without saying that not *all* uses of such techniques are irrelevant, and that they represent an indispensable moment in coming to understand contemporary music. The issue is simply this: We know that criticism ought to come only after the fact of art, but we cannot *insure* that it will come only after the fact. What is to be hoped for is that criticism learn to criticize itself, as art does, distrusting its own success.

This is particularly urgent, or perhaps particularly clear, in the case of music, because, as suggested, the absence of a strong tradition of criticism leaves this art especially vulnerable to whatever criticism becomes established, and because the recent establishment of criticism is peculiarly invulnerable to control (because of its technicalities, its scientific chic . . .). But if it is not technicality as such which is to be shunned, only, so to speak, its counterfeit, how do you tell? The moral is again, as it is in the case of the art itself: you cannot tell from outside; and the expense in getting inside is a matter for each man to go over. And again, this strict economy is not new to modern art, but only forced by it. Nor do I wish to impugn all music made with attention to "total organization," but only to dislodge the idea that what makes it legitimate is a philosophical theory—though such a theory may be needed in helping to understand the individual artistic success which alone would make it legitimate. It may be, given the velocity of our history, that the music and the theory of music illustrated in the recent work of Krenek is by now, five years later, already repudiated—not perhaps theoretically, but in fact, in the practice of those who constitute the musical world. What would this show? One may find that it shows such worries as have been expressed in this essay to be unfounded; that the fraudulent in art and the ideological in criticism will not defeat the practice of the real thing. At least they won't have this time; but that means that certain composers have in the meantime gone on writing, not only against the normal odds of art, but against the hope that the very concept of art will not be forgotten. That a few composers might, because of this distraction and discouragement, cease trying to write, is doubtless to be expected in a difficult period. But it is not unthinkable that next time all on whom the art relies will succumb to that distraction and discouragement. I do not absolutely deny, even in the face of powerful evidence, that in the end the truth will out. I insist merely that philosophy ought to help it out. Nor have I wished to suggest that the recognition of the "possibility of fraudulence" manifests itself as a permanent suspicion of all works giving themselves out as compositions or paintings or poems . . . . One *can* achieve unshakable justified faith in one's capacity to tell. I have wanted only to say that *that* is what one will have achieved.[6]

X

I have spoken of the *necessities* of the problems faced by artists of the *irreversibility* of the sequence of art styles, of the difficulties in a contemporary artist's continuing to *believe* in his work, or *mean* it. And I said it was the artist's need to maintain his own belief that forced him to give up—to the extent and in the way he has given up—the belief and response of his audience. This is reflected in literature as well, but differently. I do not mean, what I take to be obvious enough, that modern poetry often takes the making of poetry and the difficulties of poetry in the modern age, as its subject matter. What I have in mind is best exemplified in the modern theatre. The fact that the language the literary artist uses does communicate directly with his audience—in ways the contemporary "languages" of painting and music do not—was earlier taken as an advantage to the literary artist. But it is also his liability. A writer like Samuel Beckett does *not* want what is communicated easily to be what he communicates—it is not what he means. So his effort is not to find belief from his audience, but to defeat it, so that his meaning *has* to be searched for. Similarly, modern dramatists do not *rely* on their audiences, but *deny* them. Suppose an audience is thought of

[6] The addition of this paragraph is only the main, not the only, point at which a reading by the composer John Harbison caused modification or expansion of what I had written.

as "those present whom the actors ignore." Then to stop ignoring them, to recognize them explicitly, speak *to* them, insist on the fact *that* this is acting and this is a theatre, functions to remove the status of *audience* from "those out there who were ignored." Modern dramatists (e.g., Beckett, Genet, Brecht) can be distinguished by the various ways in which they deny the existences of audiences—as if they are saying: what is meant cannot be understood from that position.

But why not? Why, to raise the question in a more familiar form, can't one still write like Mozart? The question makes the obscurities and withdrawals and unappealingness of modern art seem *willful*— which is another *fact* of the experience of that art. But what is the answer to that question? One answer might be: Lots of people have written like Mozart, people whose names only libraries know; and Mozart wasn't one of them. Another answer might be: Beethoven wrote like Mozart, until he became Beethoven. Another: If Mozart were alive, he wouldn't either. Or even: The best composers do write as Mozart did (and as Bach and Beethoven and Brahms did), though not perhaps with his special fluency or lucidity. But by now that question is losing its grip, one is no longer sure what it is one was asking, nor whether these answers mean anything (which seems the appropriate consequence of looking for a simple relation between past and present). A final answer I have wanted to give is: No one *does* now write that way. But perhaps *somebody* does, living at the edge of an obscure wood, by candlelight, with a wig on. What would our response to him be? We wouldn't take him seriously as an artist? Nobody could mean such music now, be sincere in making it? And yet I've been insisting that we can no longer be sure that any artist is sincere—we haven't convention or technique or appeal to go on any longer: *anyone* could fake it. And this means that modern art, if and where it exists, *forces* the issue of sincerity, depriving the artist and his audience of every measure except absolute attention to one's experience and absolute honesty in expressing it. This is what I meant in saying that it lays bare the condition of art altogether. And of course it runs its own risks of failure, as art within established traditions does.

This will seem an unattractive critical situation to be left with. Don't we know that "the goodness or badness of poetry has nothing to do with sincerity . . . The worst love poetry of adolescents is the most sincere"?[7] But I am suggesting that we may not know what sincerity is (nor what adolescence is). The adolescent, I suppose it is assumed, has strong feelings, and perhaps some of them can be described as feelings of sincerity, which, perhaps, he attaches to the

---

[7] Rene Wellek, *A History of Modern Criticism*, Vol. II, New Haven, 1955, p. 137.

words in his poetry. Does all that make the words, his utterance in the poem, sincere? Will he, for example, *stand by them*, later, when *those* feelings are gone? Suppose he does; that will not, of course, prove that his poetry is worthwhile, nor even that it is poetry. But I haven't suggested that sincerity proves anything in particular— it can prove madness or evil as well as purity or authenticity. What I have suggested is that it shows what kind of stake the stake in modern art is, that it helps explain why one's reactions to it can be so violent, why for the modern artist the difference between artistic success and failure can be so uncompromising. The task of the modern artist, as of the modern man, is to find something he can be sincere and serious in; something he can mean. And he may not at all.

Have my claims about the artist and his audience been based on hearsay, or real evidence, or really upon the work itself? But now the "work itself" becomes a heightened philosophical concept, not a neutral description. My claims do not rest upon works of art themselves, apart from their relations to how such works are made and the reasons for which they are made, and considering that some are sincere and some counterfeit . . . . But my claim is that to know such things is to know what a work of art is—they are, if one may say so, part of its grammar. And, of course, I may be taken in.

COMMENTS

I take Cavell seriously and resist what is frankly deeper than a professional habit of registering puzzlement.

In any case, what *I* have managed to make out as his theme is some sort of variation, brought up to date, of Tolstoy's and Nietzsche's questions regarding fraudulent art (pp. 76-77). I have some remarks to make about his application of the notion of fraudulence or imposture or imitation, but I must play to some extent the role of guide through Cavell's landscape.

The telltale clues are these. Cavell remarks that modernist music distinctly, but not exclusively, raises for us the philosophical question of how we recognize genuine art—not the fake stuff, but the real thing. So he says, for instance, "You often do not know which is on trial, the object or the viewer: modern art did not invent this dilemma; it merely insists upon it" (p. 78). Earlier, he suggests that if I do not understand what modern art is all about, I may be "missing" something in *traditional* art which "they see" (critics and artists) (p. 73). Still again, he says very pointedly that one must "trust the object" of art, that "the possibility of fraudulence . . . is endemic in the experience of contemporary music," that one may in fact discover that he's been "betrayed" (p. 76). The exposure of false art requires a capacity for "recognizing something about the object itself," the same capacity needed for "recognizing the genuine article" (p. 77). And he resists the proposal that saying that this or that is an "object of art" (say, a pin or crumpled handkerchief that one might become absorbed in— think of Pop Art) is "a matter of taste" (p. 84). This brings us back to Cavell's remarks about certain paradoxical ways of speaking of our experience of art: that art is "known in sensing" (p. 78), or "known by feeling" (p. 79), that one must *tell* another what he sees in it but, of course, what is "seen" or "felt" cannot be *told* (p. 80). In a word, Cavell is concerned, as he very clearly puts it, not with a modern problem but with "the problem of modernism" (p.82). And so, he returns to the question of fraud and to the curious fact implied by the eligibility of that question—that we treat works of art rather like people—which is his gloss on Kant's well-known thesis of "purposiveness without purpose" (pp. 84-85). Art, he says, "celebrates the fact that men can *intend* their lives" (p. 85); hence, he makes much of the "virtues" of improvisation and taking advantage of chance (p. 85). In fact, he sees the venture of composing works of art and of responding to an implied "invitation" to share the "risks" of such creation as dangerous (p. 86). The price we pay, on failure, is not moral ("remorse and recompense") but "the loss of coherence altogether" (p. 86). And he traces the concept of improvisation in music in such a way as to suggest that, at the present time, the loss of traditional conventions obliges musicians (like Schoenberg and Stravinsky and Bartok) to invent new conventions (for the sake of coherence) or to risk "nihilism" and "silence," loss of communication (as in the electronic music of Stockhausen) by the "invocation of chance" and "total organization" (pp. 86-88). The former, we may suppose, provide for improvisation by performers; the latter, do not (p. 90); the implication, since there are no "shared conventions," seems to be (a little angrily put) that the new music "expresses . . . contempt for the artistic process" (p. 90). I am not always sure that this is what Cavell wishes to say, but he does hold that, if one is looking for "composition" in modern art, in painting as well as in music, the work is "absurdly trivial: a child could do it" (p. 89); and in fact "now a child *has* done it, or might as well have" (p. 91). I say I don't know whether Cavell holds this or that. But the truth is that, at the very close of his paper, asking why one can't "still write like Mozart?," he says "we wouldn't take him seriously as an artist" if he did, that "nobody could *mean* such music now, be sincere in making it" (p. 96)—which is once again the Tolstoyan theme that, *perhaps*, is the heart of the discussion.

I think it is difficult to *object* to what Cavell says, and I cannot be sure I am *opposing* anything he says. The philosophical style he employs I associate chiefly with that of John Wisdom (if I may be allowed this sort of remark). Cavell is concerned to give us part of the "grammar" of 'work of art,' (p. 97) and he has started a lot of small animals running. I think his remarks are very serious ones, though I must say that the nasty question of how I would know that this is not imitation of philosophy, rather than philosophy, crossed my mind once or twice. I was reluctant to risk myself in the sort of "trust" Cavell says is necessary in art and I frankly do not see the clear canons by appealing to which I can escape a corresponding risk.

Let me make a start at a seemingly tangential point. My clue about the new electronic music—waiving altogether, for the moment, the ideological battles that must be waged by artists *engagés*—is that composers have dispensed with the keyboard by taking the entire range of sound (now, technologically available for the first time) as their materials. They have eliminated, it is true, notation and performance and improvisation in this regard. May we say, to speak not altogether unlike Cavell, that they are

composing musical sculptures? Does saying *that* help *you* to reconsider
these compositions as works of art? Does it soften your fears of
betrayal? Is it an expression of trust? I'm not sure.

What we do when we speak this way, when we come across
genuinely puzzling things that some insist are works of art and others
insist are not, is to draw out the similarities and differences between
the new work and the old, that may exhibit the reasonableness
of construing it as art and the point of expressing some doubt.
And, by the way, Tolstoy himself—precisely in rejecting Shakespeare
and the Greeks and the rest—does draw on the canonical items of
art that no discussion can ignore. The difference, in fact, between
Tolstoy and Cavell (in at least the context of our question) is this:
Tolstoy rejects as false art a good many of the recognized paradigms
of art and what he rejects in his own contemporary period he
associates with the evil of these; Cavell is rather concerned with
how we are to know that newly minted, would-be art, that differs
significantly *from what has gone before* and is not in question in the
same sense, can be known truly *to be* art. Put another way, Tolstoy
knew the extension of 'work of art' but insisted on placing certain
preferred values of his own on particular works (calling them true or
false art); and Cavell is raising the question of how we extend the
term 'work of art' to items in a twilight zone. Tolstoy is condemning
particular works of art and Cavell is asking for special features of the
grammar of 'work of art.'

What can be said? I am inclined to insist that the logic of borderline cases is a separate philosophical issue from that of taste and
appreciation and the evaluation of objects of any sort. I quite
see that 'work of art' serves ambivalently as an honorific expression
and as a basic category allowing for valuations of different sorts.
And I quite see that fakery and imposture are serious social matters.
But it seems to me that one cannot speak of "fraud" with respect to
the *new* art (that is, would-be art that departs significantly from
the old and is called fraud *because* of that departure) in the same
sense in which one may speak of "fraud" with respect to items
produced within the scope of the informal canons that obtain, or
in the same sense in which Tolstoy addresses the tradition.

If one succeeds in laying down lines of compositional analysis
for the new art (which may well provide for random and chance
elements, as we have already done to some extent for the plastic arts,
for instance) we shall have shown the *propriety* of treating the
new music as art, in a way that is at least theoretically neutral
to condemning or praising particular works. I see nothing mysterious
here. But I do think that Cavell has used a cannon of a word
when he says that, with respect to the new art (perhaps in a sense
also appropriate within the tradition), we must be able to *recognize*

the genuine and the fraudulent. I grant that if we see no coherence in these would-be works, we cannot properly speak of art (though I am reminded of William York Tyndall's rather open admission that he had not, some years ago lecturing on Joyce, managed to read very much of *Finnegan's Wake* or to make out its plan of composition in a detailed way; and I am reminded of ardent supporters of Schoenberg who, on the occasion of his death, insisted that the analysis of certain late works *would* eventually be provided).

It is true that we need instruction about how we may construe at all the new music as music, and the instruction will concern itself with what can be discriminated in the hearing (though perhaps not exclusively: distinctions may for instance be made in musical notation that cannot be discriminated in an auditory way—are we to say that this is *not* pertinent to musical experience?). To succeed in such instruction *is* to exhibit the propriety of extending the term 'work of art' to the new items. I suggest also that "sincerity," in the sense in which Cavell introduces it, is nothing more than the implied seriousness of the artist's effort producing work that can be so construed; it has, as I see it, no independent biographical significance—which is not to say that questions of sincerity and fraud of another sort cannot be raised once the tradition of art is more or less mapped out. Perhaps Cavell has this in mind himself, for he says that professional musicians nowadays "do not quite know who is and who is not rightly included among their peers" (p. 76) and the "artist himself may not know" whether his work is fraudulent! (p. 77)

I see the somewhat mora point of Cavell's insistence on the danger of risking oneself with works of art. But betrayal, the discovery of fraud, the evaporation of apparent coherence occur, in the required sense, *within* the community of the appreciation of art. I should want to separate this matter quite carefully from that of the extension of the expression 'work of art.' Again, however, 'fraud' is a very heavy term. To use Cavell's own illustration: a man writing in the manner of Mozart today needn't be a fraud though perhaps he couldn't be taken seriously; I'm not as sure as Cavell is that *he* couldn't *mean* it (and I'm not even sure that he couldn't be taken seriously—I think of Pound working with old French forms). Cavell also suggests that "we may not know what sincerity is"—asking whether a poet will *"stand by"* his words (p. 97). I concede that I'm not entirely clear myself and invite him to spell out the notion. Nevertheless, the concepts of fraud, imposture, and imitation do have a place in the appreciation of art; and it is also true that invoking them is linked to an honorific use of the expression 'work of art.'

But perhaps the most important thing to note, in this context, is that questions of fraud, imposture, and imitation occur character-istically where the question of modernism does not; that is, within an art tradition more or less mapped out, regardless of its modernity. Consequently, I am inclined to think that Cavell has somewhat obscured his questions regarding the grasp of what is novel and what strains the tradition. The question of imposture is evaluative in some sense; that of modernism is not. Ironically, therefore, Cavell's construing modernism in terms of the genuine and the fraudulent tends to disable the problem of extending large categories, by reserving 'work of art' as an honorific term and by insisting at the same time that we must *recognize* in the *new* work what is genuine or fraudulent. One might almost say, what goes expressly against Cavell's own view, that the inclusion of the new work of art *is* a matter of taste. Certainly, on his own grounds, citing from *Die Reihe* and *Perspectives of New Music*, the case could be made out and would accord with a possible use of 'fraudulent' and 'genuine.' *I* should not wish to subscribe to such a view, but I fail to see on what grounds Cavell actually manages to dismiss it.

Finally, I think the characterization of aesthetic experience and aesthetic perception cannot be made to uncover, in any simple way, limits of attention which the efforts of the new music can be seen necessarily to violate. If an appreciation of the new music requires some knowledge of the conditions under which it is gener-ated—which is not, as such, discriminable in listening to the music—I don't understand the sense in which we may disqualify it on aesthetic grounds, as if by a *discovery* of what is relevant to aesthetic interest. I quite see that music is primarily addressed to the ear. But I don't see that *every* aesthetically relevant remark about music concerns what is heard or could be heard. I should like to know to what *sense* literature for example is directed; and I should like to know, if I compare a musical composition and a painting, in what sense I am speaking in an aesthetically irrelevant way. We are still required to mark out the audible form of a musical piece, but the interest of the new musicians in certain initial choices resulting in unpredictable auditory consequences does not, in itself, preclude the identification of audible forms (I think of automatic painting and the like) and is not, in itself, necessarily irrelevant.

COMMENTS

MONROE C. BEARDSLEY

"The dangers of fraudulence, and of trust," says Stanley Cavell, "are essential to the experience of art. If anything in this paper should count as a thesis, that is my thesis" (p. 76). The thesis is developed and discussed very interestingly, but it is not very sharply formulated—and perhaps part of what Cavell wishes to convey is that the thesis *cannot* be sharply formulated. Still, I should make an initial effort to focus what I am called upon to agree or disagree with if only to alert the author that I have missed his point entirely.

Cavell, then, I take it, holds that there is a distinction between works of art and other things, and he also holds that some things that are not works of art can be mistaken for works of art (they are in that sense "fraudulent"). These two truths are pointed up by recent artistic developments, he thinks, and a conscious awareness of them is indispensable to a full aesthetic encounter. Something like this is what I take him to be saying. So we must ask the question, "What is art?" Thus: "Is Pop Art art? Are canvasses with a few stripes or chevrons on them art?" etc. (p. 76). The problem is to clarify the distinction between works that are genuine art and those that are spurious. Perhaps this distinction cannot be made on a single principle, and we should ask instead, "What is music?," "What is poetry?," etc. Thus Cavell remarks (p. 90) that "it is not clear what is and what is not essentially connected to the concept of music." Or perhaps no general distinction at all can be made, and we can only tell in individual cases in the somewhat intuitive way Cavell describes as "knowing by feeling" (p. 79).

If the problem is one of making or marking a significant distinction, or of finding the boundaries of a species, then it begs too many questions, I think, to use the term 'fraudulence' from the start. When one thing can be mistaken for another, the problem of determining genuineness can no doubt arise, with or without the conscious deceit suggested by 'fraudulence.' Under the conditions prevailing in current music theorizing, as Cavell reviews them, it seems possible that the composer could be just as confused as anyone else about whether or not what he is writing is genuine music (*vide* Cavell, p. 77). So let me use the terms 'genuine' and 'spurious' without imputation of unworthy motives.

There is another feature of Cavell's approach that seems to me to admit or demand too much.

In emphasizing the experiences of fraudulence and of trust as essential to the experience of art, I am in effect claiming that the answer to the question "What is art?" will in part be an answer which explains why it is we treat certain objects, or how we *can* treat certain objects, in ways normally reserved for treating persons. (p. 76)

This surprises me. I don't find that I treat works of art in ways normally reserved for treating persons. And even if it is true that the experience of art necessarily involves or presupposes "trust," I don't see why we cannot direct this trust toward the artist rather than trying to treat the work itself as a person.

How can a problem about genuineness in art arise? (1) There is the risk that you might be enjoying a painting labeled El Greco or Giorgione, in (say) the Barnes Foundation, and that it might turn out to be a forgery. But that's a pseudo-peril, aesthetically speaking, since the discovery that it is a forgery does not invalidate your enjoyment if the forgery is a really good one. (2) There is the risk that you might be enjoying an abstract expressionist painting and that it might turn out to have been painted by a child or a chimpanzee or a machine. But that's a pseudo-peril, too, since the discovery that it was naively done does not invalidate your response. (3) There is the risk (which may lie hidden in the others) that you might try very hard to find something enjoyable in a painting that is strange to you, and you might just about succeed in convincing yourself that you are finding it, when you are told that there is nothing there worth looking at closely. The peril of self-deception is always with us.

The present problem arises in another way. A visitor wanders into a gallery where there are three paintings. He stands in front of the first one, which is entitled "Punch." Suddenly it opens up, and out pops a concealed metal arm with a boxing glove on the end, and hits him sharply on the nose. "Isn't there something spurious about that?" he wonders, as he moves on. The next painting assaults him in a different way. It is a large board with close wavy black lines on a white background. The catalogue reports,

> When these effects appear in certain linear and radial figures, the impression of brightness and pulsation can reach a startling intensity. The eyes seem to be bombarded with pure energy, as they are by Brigid Riley's *Current*. Even effects of colour can result—usually pale pink, gold, or blue. They are increased, Gerald Oster has determined, under the influence of the drugs mescaline and LSD.[1]

[1] William G. Seitz, *The Responsive Eye*, New York, 1965, p. 31.

Thankful that he has left his mescaline at home on this occasion, the visitor pauses to rest his heavily bombarded eyes. "I wonder if that's genuine art," he says to himself. The third painting is one of those so-called "invisible paintings" (perhaps by Ald Reinhardt). The catalogue says,

> The eyes must accommodate to the painting as they do to a dimly lit room after having been in sunlight or, conversely, as they accommodate to the transition from darkness to bright light. . . . It is easy to associate these large paintings with religious and mystical states. The contemplation of nothingness, which they invite while retaining their identity, quickly goes beyond purely visual sensation.[2]

"What am I doing here?" the visitor mutters, having come in search of visual sensations, not mystical states. Is the contemplation of nothingness, he wonders, aesthetic experience? Can nothingness be art?

Now, however easy it may be for the aesthetic reactionary to make fun, these examples really do raise issues—here I agree whole-heartedly with Cavell. I remember being in a symposium on this general topic a few years ago,[3] in which Mary Mothersill questioned this assumption. She argued with some force that the question "Is X really art?" does not arise for the serious-minded art-lover, but only for the man whose five-year-old girl could paint like Picasso if she would stoop to it and give up drawing Thanksgiving turkeys. Mothersill argued that neither this philistine nor the customs official can profit from philosophical advice about what is and what is not art; she doubted that the problem that Cavell makes central in his discussion "deserves the respectful attention" I wanted to give it. But a philosopher's horizon ought to be higher than that of a customs official, and the question "What is art?" (or the question "What is music?") still seems to me very much worth asking, in one way or another.

One answer to the question is referred to by Cavell: that is, Tolstoy's attempt to characterize what he called "counterfeit" art. It will be recalled that Tolstoy made his distinction by defining art as the transmission of lived-through feelings, and then inferring that "infection [is] a sure sign of art."[4] The degree of infectiousness was said to depend on (1) the individuality of the feeling, (2) "the clarity of the transmission," and most of all (3) "the sincerity of the artist."[5]

[2] *Ibid.*, p. 17.

[3] Beardsley, Douglas Morgan, Mary Mothersill, "On Art and the Definitions of the Arts," *Journal of Aesthetics and Art Criticism*, XX, 1961, pp. 175-198.

[4] *What Is Art?*, trans. Aylmer Maude, Oxford, 1924, p. 275.

[5] *Loc. cit.*

The absence of any one of these conditions excludes a work from the category of art and relegates it to that of art's counterfeits . . . If all these conditions are present, even in the smallest degree, then the work, even if a weak one, is yet a work of art.[6]

It is instructive, though not surprising, to see that, having made this distinction between genuine and spurious art, Tolstoy cannot manage to stick to it consistently. (After all, how could the first two conditions fail to be present in *some* degree? And how could you be sure that the third is absent?) This ambivalence is nicely reflected in Cavell's own reference to "the list of figures whose art Tolstoy dismisses as fraudulent or irrelevant or bad" (p. 80). But if it is important to distinguish genuine art from spurious art, then it is also important to know which works are to be dismissed as spurious and which as bad—since spurious art is neither good art nor bad art.

Tolstoy's criteria of genuineness fail for well-known reasons—most decisively because the sincerity of the artist is seldom verifiable. Was Shakespeare sincere when he wrote *Macbeth* or Sonnet 73? Who can say? But then we do not know whether it is genuine art or not, and if we once allow ourselves to be troubled by this question, we can never cure the trouble.

Cavell seems to want to rehabilitate the concept of sincerity, though in an altered form, a form in which, I believe, Tolstoy would not acknowledge it as *his* concept. In the crude sense, Cavell says, the artist need not be sincere; but is the adolescent love-poet *really* sincere? "Will he . . . *stand by*" his words "later, when *those* feelings are gone?" (p. 97). This is a tough test of sincerity at a particular time—that at some later time, when one no longer feels the same way, one will still "stand by" his words.

It seems to me, in fact, that Cavell draws the wrong moral about sincerity from contemporary art. On this point, he would have done better to consult Oscar Wilde than Tolstoy. "We can no longer be sure that any artist is sincere—we haven't convention or technique or appeal to go on any longer; *anyone* could fake it." (p. 96) Suppose this is true. What follows? "And this means that modern art, if and where it exists, *forces* the issue of sincerity, depriving the artist and his audience of every measure except absolute attention to one's experience and absolute honesty in expressing it." (p. 96) But how is the issue "forced"? It seems rather to me that these contemporary developments merely underline a fact that was fairly plain before, namely that sincerity is irrelevant to the proper interests and concerns of the viewer and listener. The issue is not forced, but (finally) laid to rest.

It was partly this way of interpreting current developments that

[6] *Ibid.*, p. 277.

persuaded me (in the symposium I referred to earlier) that we ought to seek a usefully objective distinction between art and non-art, i.e., between music and non-music, etc. And I proposed a few steps in this direction by trying to show that if we make any distinction at all (for example) between those sequences of sounds we wish to call music and those we do not wish to call music, we shall have to make use of certain concepts like *coherence* and *completeness*. Understandably enough, my fellow symposiasts on that occasion found little merit in this proposal, even though I tried to make it fairly definite in its application to specific forms of art. Thus, for example, I suggested that music be identified by a special sort of auditory movement, generalizing (as I thought) a famous formula of Hanslick's.

Such an attempt as this certainly begs one question that ought to be faced: Why try to define music at all? Tolstoy at least knew what he was doing, for he was a radical aesthetic reformer, and understood very well that there is no more severe way to condemn works of art than to say that they are not even art at all. But I have no such excuse. In the first place, however, one might ask: Why not define music? What if someone *does* come up with a composition for Blackboard and Ten Fingernails. Listening to three minutes of such scraping is so different from listening to the andante of *Eine Kleine Nachtmusik*, why shouldn't we give some other name than 'music' to the former? But, in the second place, there is an important use for the term 'music.' A critic, it seems to me, can say that certain music is good music and other music poor music. But if there can be a *good X*, whatever *X* may be, or a *poor X*, then there must be *X*'s. Unless we know at least roughly what class of things is marked out by a term like 'music composition,' we can't have a clear idea of what a *good* music composition or a *poor* one is. This is one reason for wanting to define the term 'music composition.'

But for this purpose, of course, it is enough to give the term 'music' a broad sense that will accommodate anything that anyone could possibly have any excuse for calling music. This sense can be achieved by a two-stage definition, worked out in the following way.

To begin with, we may take *sequences of sounds* as our genus. Some of these sequences are characterized, as I have said, by a special sort of coherence or continuity, which is auditory movement. These are (roughly) those sequences that have rhythm and/or melody. Let us say that any sound-sequence with auditory movement is "music (narrowly speaking)."[7] The class of musical compositions that are music in this sense contains the uncontested works, those that would clearly have to be included in the denotation of 'music' by any appropriate definition.

[7] This is the sense I tried to clarify in the symposium referred to above.

To reach the second stage, we need another concept that cuts across the first. Consider sequences of sounds as produced for sustained auditory attention—by presenting them to an audience, by asking for respectful listening, by framing them with antecedent silence, by recording found noises and making them available for reproduction, etc. Let us say that in these and similar cases the sequence of sounds is "exhibited." The analogies for the exhibition of paintings, plays, poems, sculptural constructions, and so forth, are perhaps evident enough. To exhibit is to segregate from the environment in some way, to some degree—to assign a context that permits comparatively undivided attention, and hence to invite (or at least make possible) aesthetic experiencing.

We can now let 'music (broadly speaking)' refer to those sound-sequences that either have auditory movement or are exhibited. Then the Composition for Blackboard and Ten Fingernails, when performed, is music (broadly speaking). The question remains open, of course, whether it is *good* music. And the question can still lead into many of the difficult concerns of aesthetics. But the problem of *spurious* music no longer arises. Not that there is no such thing as non-music (for many things are not music). But no sound-sequence can be offered as music that really isn't, since to offer it is to make it music (broadly speaking).

It is instructive, I think, to compare the task of defining music (or any of the arts) with the task of defining 'deductive argument.' If we are going to have a concept like *deductive argument*, without which we shall not be able to use the convenient term 'invalid deductive argument,' we have to reach this concept by a similar two-stage definition. First, we take the concept of *following necessarily*, by means of which we can define 'valid argument.' Next we form the class of arguments that *purport* to be valid, whether they are or not— arguments that are offered with an internal or contextual claim that the conclusion follows necessarily from the reason. This is not, or not primarily, a matter of intention: we have a range of cues or clues that can embody this claim, including the shape of the argument itself (if it is a syllogism, whose structure is pointed up, we take that as a hint that it claims to be a *valid* syllogism.) Then we can define 'deductive argument' as "argument that either is valid or is asserted (by overt statement or by implicit suggestion) to be valid."

The analogy between defining 'deductive argument' and defining 'music (broadly speaking)' is no more complete than most analogies but it suggests some reflections. First, we could evidently get along without the concept of *deductive argument*, despite its pedagogical usefulness, and, when we are confronted with an argument, simply inquire whether it is valid or not. Similarly, we could get along without the concept of *music (broadly speaking)*, and inquire of every sequence of sounds that comes our way whether it does or does not achieve the coherence of auditory movement. Second, the concept of *deductive argument* helps conserve our critical energies, by directing our attention particularly to those arguments that have *prima facie* deductiveness, that seem to deserve consideration from what might be called the "validity point of view." Similarly, the concept of *music (broadly speaking)* reminds us that there is not much point in asking of all the noises we hear whether they are music, but that there are certain sound—sequences that may be rewarding if approached from the *musical* point of view. But third, the concept of *deductive argument* may have the disadvantage of underemphasizing the important fact that when an argument turns out to be invalid, that is not the end of our interest in it from a logical point of view, for we must also ask whether or not it is a good *inductive* argument for its conclusion. But the concept of *music (broadly speaking)* has precisely the advantage of stressing the continuity between what all take to be music and those adventurous experiments in composition that explore the borders of music (narrowly speaking) and other sounds.

There is one possible objection to this broad concept of music, as far as I can see, and it is touched on by Cavell. One could say that the whole point of raising the question of genuiness in art is that the problematic works cannot be assimilated to the unproblematic ones, that my imaginary Composition cannot be judged by any standards applicable to Mozart's *Serenade*; or, as Cavell puts it, "that such works cannot be *criticized*, as traditional art is criticized, but must be defended, or rejected as art altogether" (p. 83). But I take it that Cavell does not accept this view himself, for he says that "such philosophizing as Krenek's . . . must not be used to protect [the activity of producing such works] against aesthetic assessment" (p. 83). Then we are in agreement on this important point, I am glad to say. In that case, however, there is no *a priori* bar to regarding any exhibited sequence of sounds from what might be called the "aesthetic point of view"—that is, listening for any traces of musical worth that it might possess: patterns of inner relationship that give it shape, notable regional qualities that give it character. I don't know that a music listener who came to consider music in this light—always inquiring after the better and the worse rather than after the authentic and the fake—would necessarily be missing something valuable in art. In one way he would certainly be naïve, but perhaps his naïveté would be of the angelic sort. And this innocent might get more out of his aesthetic life than someone who is always worried that he is being had. So if it *is* the thesis of Cavell's paper that "the dangers of fraudulence, and of trust, are essential to the experience of art" (p. 76), then I think the thesis is probably not true.

REJOINDERS

STANLEY CAVELL

I

It is not surprising that Professors Beardsley and Margolis found what I had to say about modern art and modern philosophy obscure and, I take it, unsympathetic; I tried, in the opening section of my remarks, to give reasons why these subjects are liable to obscurity and unattractiveness—as it were, to make this fact itself a subject of philosophy. (In perhaps the way Hume suggests, in the Introduction to his *Dialogues on Natural Religion*, that the subject to follow is characterized by alternating obscurity and obviousness.) It is therefore the more surprising that they find me clear enough to agree in several points of interpretation and in one or two major proposals. (1) Both take it as a central motive of my paper to rule out certain developments within recent music as genuine art. (2) Both object to my insistence on the word 'fraudulence,' wishing some more neutral description. (3) Accepting the fact that objects of modern art create a problem for aesthetics, but taking the nature of that problem as known, each suggests an alternate line of solution, and in each case the solution is one which is, and is explicitly said to be, philosophically familiar: Beardsley's solution is to define a notion of art (i.e., music) broad enough to include the problematic objects; Margolis' is to regard the problem as another instance of "borderline cases" and therefore to require the discovery of criteria for the "propriety" of treating the new music as art. (4) Both suggest that an obvious notion of organization or coherence will supply the (or a) determining ground for including objects under the new classification.

These are not my problems. Taking them in order:

(1) I was not directly concerned to rule out or rule in any partic- ular work as music, but to bring to attention the fact that this had become a problem in modern art and to suggest that it therefore ought to become a problem for philosophy. I do not think it is clear, and I found it of philosophical interest that it is not clear, what kind of problem modern art poses, nor what philosophical considerations might uncover it. But I am confident that the redefinition or extended application of the term 'music' is not what is needed, for that leaves the behavior of composers and critics and audiences and the experience of the works themselves, old and

new, incomprehensible—a problem has not been solved, but made invisible. Convinced that swans are white, and one day stopped by a black bird for all the world a swan, I have some freedom: "So I was wrong"; I learned something. "So there is a swan-like bird which is black"; but then I had better have a good reason for taking color to be so important. But in the present case it is as though there is something on the horizon which *for some reason* I insist on calling swans (and after all, it isn't as though I *knew* the reasons, or even had reasons, for calling the old ones swans), but which sometimes look and behave so differently that not only do I feel called on to justify *their* title, I feel called on to justify my hitherto unquestioned ability to recognize the old ones. How do I do it; what *is* it about them? Surely that graceful neck is essential—its melodic line, so to speak? But it may be that my experience of the new ones makes the old neck rather a distasteful feature sometimes, as though it were somehow arbitrary, as though the old ones now sometimes look *bent*.

(2) Similarly, I was not directly concerned to condemn any given work as fraudulent, but to call attention to (what I took to be) the obvious but unappreciated *fact* that the experience of the modern is one which itself raises the question of fraudulence and genuineness (in something like the way I take the experience of momentary or extended irrelevance, and sudden relevance, to be characteristic of philosophy; the way the experience, and danger, of the distance or absence of God, and sudden closeness, is characteristic of modern religion). It goes without saying that I may be wrong about this experience, or poor in characterizing it and sounding its significance. But if I am not wrong, then the problems it raises, or ought to raise, are not touched by suggesting that I am unjustly attributing motives to certain artists, nor by redefining terms in such a way that the attribution of fraudulence need not or cannot arise. For the experience itself has the form of attributing motives (I referred, for example, to the riots and inner violence which dog the history of the *avant garde*), and redefining some terms will not, or ought not, make the experience go away.

(3) What ought to make the experience go away? Further experience, or else nothing; entering the new world of these objects, understanding them not in theory but as objects of art, in the sense in which we have always, when we have ever, understood such objects.[1] This is the essential reason that redefinitions and borderline cases are irrelevant here. For the question raised for me about these new objects is exactly whether they are, and how they can be,

---

[1] I have adumbrated relations between this problem (with specific attention to the development of post-tonal music) and Wittgenstein's notions of "grammar" and "forms of life," in "Aesthetic Problems of Modern Philosophy," a contribution to *Philosophy in America*, ed. Max Black, London and Ithaca, N. Y., 1965.

central. If they are not, if I cannot in that way enter their world, I do not know what interest, if any at all, I would have in them. It *may* turn out to be one which would prompt me to think of them as borderline cases of art; or I might think of them as something which replaces (which replaces my interest in) works of art.

Not every object will raise this question of art, i.e., raise the question "What is art?" by raising the question "Is this, e.g., music?" Pop Art as a whole does not, and it is exactly part of its intention and ideology that it should not. For philosophy to scramble for definitions which accommodate these objects unproblematically as art—or art in a wide sense, or borderline cases of art—insures its irrelevance, taking seriously neither the claims such objects make (*sc.*, that they are not art) nor the specialized amusements such objects can provide (e.g., a certain theatricality), nor the attitude they contain toward serious art (*sc.*, that it is past); nor the despair under the fun, the nihilism under the comment, nor the cultural-philosophical confusion which makes such claims and fun and comment possible.

And not every new work which gives itself out as serious art will raise the question of art. Part of what I say in my paper is a function of the fact that, for me, Krenek's late work does not raise this question, and that, for example, Caro's sculpture does. It is not, in this context, important whether I am right or wrong about these particular cases; what is important here is what kind of issue this issue is, what I would be right or wrong about.

It is, first of all, an issue in which it is *up to me* (and, of course, up to you) whether an object does or does not count as evidence for any theory I am moved to offer; and 'count as evidence' means "count as art at all." Both Beardsley and Margolis wish explicitly to separate the question of evaluation from the question of classification. Now I might define the problem of modernism as one in which the question of value comes first as well as last: to classify a modern work as art is already to have staked value, more starkly than the (later) decision concerning its goodness or badness. Your interest in Mozart is not likely to draw much attention—which is why such interests can be, so to speak, academic. But an interest in Webern or Stockhausen or Cage is, one might say, revealing, even sometimes suspicious. (A Christian might say that in such interests, and choices, the heart is revealed. This is what Tolstoy saw.) Philosophers sometimes speak of the phrase 'work of art' as having an "honorific sense," as though that were a surprising or derivative fact about it, even one to be neutralized or ignored. But that works of art are valuable is analytically true of them; and that value is inescapable in human experience and conduct is one of the facts of life, and of art, which modern art lays bare.

Of course there is the continuous danger that the question will be begged, that theory and evidence become a closed and vicious circle. I do not insist that this is always the case, but merely that unless this problem is faced here no problem of the right kind can come to focus. For if everything counted as art which now offers itself as art, then questions about whether, for example, figurative content, or tonality, or heroic couplets are still viable resources for painters, composers, and poets would not only never have arisen, but would make no sense. When there was a tradition, everything which seemed to count did count. (And that is perhaps analytic of the notion of "tradition.") I say that Krenek's late work doesn't count, and that means that the way it is "organized" does not raise for me the question of how music may be organized. I say that Caro's steel sculptures count, and that raises for me the question of what sculpture is: I had—I take it everyone had—thought (assumed? imagined?—but no one word is going to be quite right, and that must itself require a philosophical account) that a piece of sculpture was something *worked* (carved, chipped, polished, etc.); but Caro uses steel rods and beams and sheets which he does not work (e.g., bend or twist) but rather, one could say, *places*. I had thought that a piece of sculpture had the coherence of a natural object, that it was what I wish to call spatially closed or spatially continuous (or consisted of a group of objects of such coherence); but a Caro may be open and discontinuous, one of its parts not an outgrowth from another, nor even joined or connected with another so much as it is juxtaposed to it, or an inflection from it. I had thought a piece of sculpture stood on a base (or crouched in a pediment, etc.) and rose; but a Caro rests on the raw ground and some do not so much rise as spread or reach or open. I had heard that sculpture used to be painted, and took it as a matter of fashion or taste that it no longer was (in spite of the reconstructed praises of past glories, the idea of painted stone figures struck me as ludicrous); Caro paints his pieces, but not only is this not an external or additional fact about them, it creates objects about which I wish to say they are not painted, or not *colored*: they have color not the way, say, cabinets or walls do, but the way grass and soil do—the experience I recall is perhaps hit off by saying that Caro is not using colored beams, rods, and sheets, but beams and rods and sheets of color. It is almost as though the color helps de-materialize its supporting object. One might wish to say they are weightless, but that would not mean that these massively heavy materials seem light, but, more surprisingly, neither light nor heavy, resistant to the concept of weight altogether—as they are resistant to the concept of size; they seem neither large nor small. Similarly, they seem to be free of *texture*, so critical a parameter of other sculpture. They are no longer *things*.[2] (Something similar seems to be true of the use of color in recent painting: it is not merely that it no longer serves as the color *of* something, nor that it is disembodied; but that the canvas we know to underly it is no longer its *support*—the color is simply *there*, as the canvas is. How it got there is only technically (one could say it is no longer humanly) interesting; it is no longer *handled*.)

The problem this raises for me is exactly not to decide whether this is art (I mean, sculpture), nor to find some definition of 'sculpture' which makes the Caro pieces borderline cases of sculpture, or sculptures in some extended sense. The problem is that I am, so to speak, stuck with the knowledge that this is sculpture, in the same sense that any object is. The problem is that I no longer know what sculpture is, why I call *any* object, the most central or traditional, a piece of sculpture. How *can* objects made this way elicit the experience I had thought confined to objects made so differently? And that this is a matter of experience is what needs constant attention; nothing more, but nothing less, than that. Just as it needs constant admission that one's experience may be wrong, or misformed, or inattentive and inconstant.

This admission is more than a reaffirmation of the first fact about art, that it must be felt, not merely known—or, as I would rather put it, that it must be known for oneself. It is a statement of the fact of life—the metaphysical fact, one could say—that apart from one's experience of it there is nothing to *be* known about it, no way of knowing that what you know is relevant. For what else is there for me to rely on but my experience? It is only if I accept (my experience of) the Caro that I have to conclude that the art of sculpture does not (or does no longer) depend on figuration, on being worked, on spatial continuity, etc. Then what does it depend on? That is, again, the sort of issue which prompted me to say that modern art lays bare the condition of art in general. Or put it this way: That an object is "a piece of sculpture" is not (no longer) grammatically related to its "being sculptured," i.e., to its being the result of carving or chipping, etc., some material with some tool. Then we no longer know what kind of object a piece of sculpture (grammatically) is. That it is not a natural object is something we knew. But it also is not an artifact either—or if it is, it is one which defines no known craft. It is, one would like to say, a work of art. But what is it one will then be saying?

---

[2] In addition to the piece on Caro cited in note 5 of my opening paper, see also Fried's catalogue essay for an exhibition of Caro's work at the Whitechapel Art Gallery, London, September-October 1963; and Clement Greenberg's "The New Sculpture" and "Modernist Sculpture, Its Pictorial Past," both in his *Art and Culture* (Boston), 1961.

Two serious ambiguities in my initial paper become particularly relevant here:

(a) Beardsley, with good reason, on several occasions is puzzled about whether I am addressing the question "Is this music?" or "Is this (music) art?" I was, and am, very uncertain about this important alternation; but I want to suggest what it is I am uncertain about and why I take it to be important.

There is this asymmetry between the questions: If there is a clear answer to the question, "Is this music (painting, sculpture . . .)?," then the question whether it is art is irrelevant, superfluous. If it is music then (analytically) it is art. That seems unprejudicial. But the negation does not: If it is not music then it is not art. But why does that seem prejudicial? Why couldn't we allow Pop Art, say, or Cage's evenings, or Happenings, to be entertainments of some kind without troubling about art? But we are troubled. Because for us, given the gradual self-definitions and self-liberations over the past century of the separate major arts we accept, Pop Art presents itself as, or as challenging, painting; Cage presents his work as, or as challenging the possibility of, music . . . . It would be enough to say that objects of Pop Art are not paintings or sculptures, that works of Cage and Krenek are not music—*if* we are clear what a painting is, what a piece of music is. But the trouble is that the genuine article—the music of Schoenberg and Webern, the sculpture of Caro, the painting of Morris Louis, the theatre of Brecht and Beckett—really does challenge the art of which it is the inheritor and voice. Each is, in a word, not merely modern, but modernist. Each, one could say, is trying to find the limits or essence of its own procedures. And this means that it is not clear *a priori* what counts, or will count, as a painting, or sculpture or musical composition . . . . So we haven't got clear criteria for determining whether a given object is or is not a painting, a sculpture . . . . But this is exactly what our whole discussion has prepared us for. The task of the modernist artist, as of the contemporary critic, is to find what it is his art finally depends upon; it doesn't matter that we haven't *a priori* criteria for defining a painting, what matters is that we realize that the criteria are something we must discover, discover in the continuity of painting itself. But my point now is that to discover this we need to discover what objects we *accept* as paintings, and why we so accept them. And to "accept something as a painting" is to "accept something as a work of art," i.e., as something carrying the intentions and consequences of art: the nature of the acceptance is altogether crucial. So the original questions "Is this music?" and "Is this art?" are not independent. The latter shows, we might say, the spirit in which the former is relevantly asked.

(b) To say that the modern "lays bare" may suggest that there was something concealed in traditional art which hadn't, for some reason, been noticed, or that what the modern throws over—tonality, perspective, narration, the absent fourth wall, etc.—was something inessential to music, painting, poetry, and theatre in earlier periods. These would be false suggestions.[3] For it is not that now we finally know the true condition of art; it is only that someone who does not question that condition has nothing, or not the essential thing, to go on in addressing the art of our period. And far from implying that we now know, for example, that music does not require tonality, nor painting figuration nor theatre an audience of spectators, etc., exactly what I want to have accomplished is to make all such notions problematic, to force us to ask, for example, what the art was which as a matter of fact did require, or exploit, tonality, perspective, etc. Why did it? What made such things media of art? It may help to say that the notion of "modernism laying bare its art" is meant not as an interpretation of history (the history of an art), but as a description of the latest period of a history, a period in which each of the arts seems to be, even forced to be, drawing itself to its limits, purging itself of elements which can be foregone and which therefore seem arbitrary or extraneous—poetry wishing the abstraction and immediacy of lyricism; theatre wishing freedom from entertainment and acting; music wishing escape from the rhythm or logic of the single body and its frame of emotion . . . . *Why* this has happened one would like to know, but for the moment what is relevant is that it has happened at a certain moment in history. For it was not always true of a given art that it sought to keep its medium pure, that it wished to assert its own limits, and therewith its independence of the other arts. Integrity could be assured without purity. So in saying that "we do not know what is and what is not essentially connected to the concept of music" I am not saying that what we do not know is which one or more phenomena are always essential to something's being music, but that we have yet to discover what at any given moment has been essential to our accepting something as music. As was said, this discovery is unnecessary as long as there is a tradition—when everything which is offered for acceptance is the real thing. But so far as the possibility of fraudulence is characteristic of the modern, then the need for a grounding of our acceptance becomes an issue for aesthetics. I think of it as a need for an answer to the question, What is a medium of art?

Philosophers will sometimes say that sound is the medium of

[3] Sources of these suggestions, and ways they are false, were brought out by Michael Fried in his course of lectures on Nineteenth Century French Painting, given at Harvard in the spring term of 1965-66.

music, paint of painting, wood and stone of sculpture, words of literature. One has to find what problems have been thought to reach illumination in such remarks. What needs recognition is that wood or stone would not be a medium of sculpture *in the absence of the art of sculpture*. The home of the idea of a *medium* lies in the visual arts, and it used to be informative to know that a given medium is oil or gouache or tempera or dry point or marble . . . because each of these media had characteristic possibilities, an implied range of handling and result. The idea of a medium is not simply that of a physical material, but of a material-in-certain-characteristic-applications. Whether or not there is anything to be called, and any good purpose in calling anything, "the medium of music," there certainly are things to be called various media of music, namely the various ways in which various sources of sound (from and for the voice, the several instruments, the body, on different occasions) have characteristically been applied: the media are, for example, plain song, work song, the march, the fugue, the aria, dance forms, sonata form. It is the existence or discovery of such strains of convention that have made possible musical expression—presumably the role a medium was to serve. In music, the "form" (as in literature, the genre) is the medium. It is within these that composers have been able to speak and to intend to speak, performers to practice and to believe, audiences to attend and to know. Grant that these media no longer serve, as portraits, nudes, odes, etc., no longer serve, for speaking and believing and knowing. What now is a medium of music? If one wishes now to answer, "Sound. Sound itself," that will no longer be the neutral answer it seemed to be, said to distinguish music from, say, poetry or painting (whatever it means to "distinguish" things one would never have thought could be taken for one another); it will be one way of distinguishing (more or less tendentiously) music now from music in the tradition, and what it says is that there are no longer known structures which must be followed if one is to speak and be understood. The medium is to be discovered, or invented out of itself.

If these sketches and obscurities are of any use, they should help to locate, or isolate, the issue of Pop Art, which is really not central to the concerns of my paper. Left to itself it may have done no harm, its amusements may have remained clean. But it was not made to be left to itself, any more than pin ball games or practical jokes or starlets are; and in an artistic-philosophical-cultural situation in which mass magazines make the same news of it they make of serious art, and in which critics in elite magazines underwrite such adventures—finding new bases for aesthetics and a new future for art in every new and safe weirdness or attractiveness which catches on—it is worth saying: This is not painting; and it is not painting not because paintings *couldn't* look like that, but because serious painting doesn't; and it doesn't, not because serious painting is not forced to change, to explore its own foundations, even its own look; but because the *way* it changes—what will count as a relevant change—is determined by the commitment to painting as an *art*, in struggle with the history which makes it an art, continuing and countering the conventions and intentions and responses which comprise that history. It may be that the history of a given art has come to an end, a very few centuries after it has come to a head, and that nothing more can be said and meant in terms of that continuity and within those ambitions. It is as if the various anti-art movements claim to *know* this has happened and to provide us with distraction, or to substitute new gratifications for those well gone; while at the same time they claim the respect due only to those whose seriousness they cannot share; and they receive it, because of our frightened confusion. Whereas such claims, made from such a position, are no more to be honored than the failed fox's sour opinion about the grapes.

(4) I have been saying that what the modern puts in question is not merely, so to speak, itself, but its tradition as a whole. Without allowing this to become problematic, one will, for example, suppose that "organization" of some more or less indefinite description, is essential to art. So I used Krenek and Caro as examples which I hoped would bring that supposition into question: If Krenek's work fails to be music, this proves not merely that "organization" is not a sufficient condition of art—which we ought to have learned from Beckmesser as well as from his progeny; it suggests that we do not know what to look for as organizing a piece of music, nor what the point of any particular organization is supposed to be. Since Caro's work succeeds in being sculpture, the received notion of organization pales in a more obvious way: I do not say that it has become completely irrelevant but only that it is completely problematic. So far as "organization" just means "composition," his pieces have about the same degree of organization as a three-legged stool. (Some will suppose that therefore a three-legged stool is a candidate for sculpture, and exhibit it. Well and good; look one over.) To say what "organization" in fact refers to in his work would be to say what organization consists in there.

II

Whatever the distances between our philosophical and aesthetic sensibilities and tolerances, there are several further points at which it still seems to me reasonable to have hoped that what I wrote would have helped my commentators to some caution with their several certainties. Margolis makes me say, and say "angrily," that " . . . the new music 'expresses . . . contempt for the artistic process' " (p. 99); whereas what I said expressed this contempt was not "the new music," but two particular *theories* or apologies which are offered in defense of certain new music (cf. p. 90). This slip is distressing, because the oblique and shifting relations between an art, and its criticism, and philosophy, is a major theme of the entire paper. Having summarized me, he begins his objections by (a) mentioning "the ideological battles which must be waged by artists *engagés*," and (b) taking it as his "clue about the new electronic music that composers have dispensed with the keyboard by taking the entire range of sound (now technologically available for the first time) as their materials." He concedes (c) that "they have eliminated . . . notation and performance and impro-visation in this regard," suggesting that they are "composing musical sculptures" (pp. 99-100). Taking these points in turn: (a) In what sense are composers and painters *engagés*, and why *must* ideological battles be waged by them? I suggested that composers, in obvious ways the least *engagés* of artists (in the normal, lately fashionable sense of that term), had become the most embattled artistically, and I took this as characteristic of the musical community now. To say, as if it is obvious, that artists "must" wage ideological battles, obscures the particular phenomenon I wanted to make surprising, that composers have come to feel compelled to defend their work in theoretical papers, a phenomenon I take, in turn, to be characteristic of the kind of work they are compelled to produce. It is, moreover, a phenomenon that has a recognizable and datable beginning in its modern form, with Wagner's writings in the middle of the nineteenth century. (b) To speak, as if in explanation, and with satisfaction, of "the entire range of sound now technologically available" is simply to accept the cant of one of the embattled positions, with no suggestion as to why that position has been opted for. (c) In *what* regard have notation, performance, and improvisation *not* been eliminated; and is this elimination of significance? When Margolis goes on to ask whether what is thereby "composed" may be called "musical sculptures," he astonishingly turns to the reader to find the answer, instead of giving his own; but since his phrase is baked up for the occasion, and since the only point in serving it would be to express an insight or temptation he has discovered in himself and therefore wishes us to test in ourselves, what can one conclude from his avoiding any response to it, but that there was nothing on his mind? So he has in fact given *no* suggestion about how this new access of the entire range of sound may or may not relate to music.

It may be true, as Beardsley says, that "Tolstoy at least knew what he was doing, for he was a radical aesthetic reformer, and understood very well that there is no more severe way to condemn works of art than to say that they are not even art at all" (p. 107). But one is not confident that Tolstoy's motives in his writings about art are justly seen when they are put as "condemning works of art"; for first, Tolstoy's point is that these works are not art, and second, he is condemning far more than putative works of art. Moreover, his condemnations seem mild compared to other ways in which art can be condemned, e.g., politically or religiously or simply through steady indifference—indeed, one of his motives, perhaps the most fundamental, was exactly to rescue genuine art (on anybody's view) from its condemnation to irrelevance, or to serving as morsels for the overstuffed, or as excitements for those no longer capable of feeling. Whatever Tolstoy understood very well, the denial that certain putative works of art are art at all is a criticism characteristic of, only available to criticism within, the modern period of art, beginning in the nineteenth century. Apart from Tolstoy and Nietzsche, other representative figures in this line would be Kierkegaard and Baudelaire, and Ruskin and Arnold.

III

I had wanted to bring more data to the issues of intention and seriousness and sincerity, but Beardsley finds that the phenomena which I say force the issue of intention, instead finally lay it to rest (p. 106). Here we do seem flatly incomprehensible to one another. However intractable the issue has been, one is dragged back over it again, faced with the alternatives Beardsley proposes: what we are to notice in "music (narrowly speaking)" is, roughly, rhythm and/or melody (p. 107); and what we are to listen for in "music (broadly speaking)"—i.e., in that part of it which is not music (narrowly speaking)—are "any traces of musical worth" (p. 109). I find that I can imagine listening to almost anything (which is audible, or in motion) for some trace of musical worth— except precisely those works which I accept as *music* (unless the context is one in which I am convinced that a piece of music is for the most part without a trace of musical worth). "Musical worth" is explained as "patterns of inner relationship that give it shape, notable regional qualities that give it character" (p. 109). But one can find or produce things of that description virtually at will, e.g., with hand claps, feet taps, and the sound of spoons tinkling; I am not on such grounds moved to call them music, however

entertaining the proceedings. (They may be *related* to music in various
ways, e.g., the way a design, say of a room, may be related to
some painting.) What is missing from the characterizations of
both the narrow and the broad is the sense that the thing one
is listening to, listening for, is the *point* of the piece. And to know
its point is to know the answer to a sense of the question "Why is it
as it is?" It *bears explanation*, not perhaps the way tides and depres-
sions do, but the way remarks and actions do. And a question I
meant to be raising in my paper was: Is there any reason other than
philosophical possession which should prevent us from saying,
what seems most natural to say, that such questions discover the
artist's intention in a work? I gave a number of reasons for thinking
that the philosophical prohibition against saying this is poorly or
obscurely conceived, and others meant to show why it seems lucidly
true, i.e., cases in which it is in fact right. The appeal to intention
can *in fact* be inappropriate or distracting or evasive, as it can in
moral contexts; no doubt it frequently is in some of the work of
the literary historians and aestheticians opposed by the New
Criticism. It is one irony of recent literary history that the New
Criticism, with one motive fixed on preserving poetry from what it
felt as the encroachment of science and logical positivism (repeating
as an academic farce what the nineteenth century went through
as a cultural tragedy), accepted undemurringly a view of intention
established, or pictured, in that same philosophy—according to
which an intention is some internal, prior mental event causally
connected with outward effects, which remain the sole evidence
for its having occurred.

This seems to underlie the following sort of remark: "Tolstoy's
criteria of genuineness fail for well-known reasons—most decisively
because the sincerity of the artist is seldom verifiable. Was Shakespeare sincere when he wrote *Macbeth* or Sonnet 73? Who can say?"
(p. 106) Is that a rhetorical question? And does it mean,
What difference does it make? But why ask it rhetorically? When
I said that modern art forced the question of seriousness and
intention and sincerity, I thought the implication clear enough
that the issue was not *forced* in earlier art, and I suggested reasons
for that: e.g., that conventions were deep enough to achieve
conviction without private backing. If the question is a real one,
what is the answer? Is it that *nobody* can say, because there is no
verification available for any answer? But that assumes we know
what "verification" would look like here. Beardsley refers to
"well-known reasons" for the failure of such considerations. He
may have in mind the sort of considerations pressed by him and
W. K. Wimsatt in their well-known article, "The Intentional
Fallacy":

One must ask how a critic expects to get an answer to the question about intention. How is he to find out what the poet tried to do? If the poet succeeded in doing it, then the poem itself shows what he was trying to do. And if the poet did not succeed, then the poem is not adequate evidence, and the critic must go outside the poem—for evidence of an intention that did not become effective in the poem.[4]

It is still worth saying about such remarks that they appeal to a concept of intention as relevant to art which does not exist elsewhere: in, for example, the case of ordinary conduct, nothing is more *visible* than actions which are not meant, visible *in* the slip, the mistake, the accident, the inadvertence . . . , and by what follows (the embarrassment, confusion, remorse, apology, attempts to correct . . .). Of course we may not know what is happening in a given case: the boxer who connects and wins may have meant to miss and throw the fight. We may have to go outside the punch itself to find this out, but then there is no question what kind of evidence will be relevant. Now, how is it imagined we are to discover the artist's intention—when, that is, we are told that there is no way inside the poem of verifying it? Are we supposed to *ask* the poet, or interview someone who knows him well? But the problem is: how is anything we learn in such ways to be identified as the intention of *this* work?

I had suggested that a certain sense of the question "Why this?" is essential to criticism, and that the "certain sense" is characterized as one in which we are, or seem to be, asking about the artist's intention in the work. If this is correct, then these are plain facts, true descriptions which depend on knowing what kind of objects poems are and what kind of activity criticism is. The philosopher, hearing such claims and descriptions, has his ancient choice: he can repudiate them, on the ground that they *cannot* be true (because of his philosophical theory—in this case of what poems are and what intentions are and what criticism is); or he can accept them as data for his philosophical investigation, learning from them what it is his philosophizing must account for. Beardsley's procedure is the former, mine the latter. According to Beardsley's, when a critic inquires about intention, seriousness, sincerity, etc., he is forced outside the work. My point is that he finds this true because of his idea of where an intention is to be searched for, and because he has been reading unhelpful critics. For the *fact* is that the correct sense of the question "Why?" directs you further *into* the work.

[4] "The Intentional Fallacy," in W. K. Wimsatt, *The Verbal Icon*, New York, 1954, p. 4.

In saying that this, if true, is a fact, I mean to be saying that it is no more than a fact; it is not an *account* of objects of art, and intention, and criticism, which shows the role of this fact in our dealings with art.

I said that it is not merely a bad picture of intention that makes this seem false or contentious or paradoxical, it is also a bad picture of what a poem is. It is the picture of a poem as more or less like a physical object,[5] whereas the first fact of works of art is that they are meant, meant to be understood.[6] A poem, whatever else it is, is an *utterance* (outer-ance). It is as true to say of poems that they are physical objects as to say of human actions that they are physical motions (though it is perfectly true that there would not be an action unless somebody moved, did something). But it is pointless to pursue this discussion in the absence of concrete instances of works and criticism to which each philosophy undertakes responsibility. So let me simply claim that apart from the recognition that one's subject, in art, is the intentionality of objects, one will appeal, in speaking of these objects, to sources of organization (rhyme schemes, scansion patterns, Baroque "structure," sonata "form," etc.) in ways which fail to tell why *this* thing is as it is, how it means what it does.

But of course I was claiming, in my paper, more than this. I was claiming that in modernist art the issue of the artist's intention, his seriousness and his sincerity, has taken on a more naked role in our acceptance of his works than in earlier periods. This is an empirical claim, depending on a view of the recent history of the arts and on my experience of individual works of that period. I discussed the concept of intention only long enough to try to head off the use of a philosophical theory which would prevent, or

---

[5] "Judging a poem is like judging a pudding or a machine. One demands that it work. It is only because an artifact works that we infer the intention of an artificer. 'A poem should not mean but be.' A poem can *be* only through its *meaning*—since its medium is words—yet it *is*, simply, *is*, in the sense that we have no excuse for inquiring what part is intended or meant." *Ibid.*, p. 4.

[6] Someone will feel: "No. The first fact about works of art is that they are *sensuous*—their impact is immediate, not intellectual." There are times when that will be what needs emphasis, because that will be the thing we have forgotten. And I do not wish to deny what it means. But it only says why there is a problem. If words always supplied only information, if paintings were always diagrams or illustrations, if music were always the heightening of serious, or light, occasions; there would be no problem (or not the same problem) about whether, or how, the work is meant. Again, it should be considered that this emphasis on sensuousness is fully true only during certain moments in the arts, for example when pleasure is its motivation (when, say, gardening was still considered, as in Kant, one of the arts; and that motivation, in varying intensities, will no doubt continue in the major arts when gardens and gardening no longer serve it sufficiently). Still, if one wishes: The first question of aesthetics is: How does that (sensuous object) mean anything?

prejudice, an investigation of this claim. In this, I was evidently unsuccessful. So let me give one further suggestion about why, if the considerations I raised are relevant, they have not been confronted.

The New Critics' concentration on the poem itself, in a way which made the poet's intention or sincerity look irrelevant, had an immediate liability in their relative neglect of Romantic poets and their successors. (In itself, this is hardly surprising: particular poetic theories are directly responsive to *certain* poetic practice.) My claim can be put by saying that the practice of poetry alters in the nineteenth and twentieth centuries, in such a way that the issues of intention and seriousness and sincerity are forced upon the reader by the poem itself: the relation between author and audience alters (because the relation between the author and his work alters, because the relation between art and the rest of culture alters . . .). Specifically, the practice of art—not merely the topic of art, but as it were the replacing or internalizing of its pervasive topic—becomes religious. When Luther said, criticizing one form in which the sacraments had become relics, "*All* our experience of life should be baptismal in character," he was voicing what would become a guiding ambition of Romanticism—when religious forms could no longer satisfy that ambition. Baudelaire characterizes Romanticism as, among other things, intimacy and spirituality. This suggests why it is not merely the threat of fraudulence and the necessity for trust which has become characteristic of the modern, but equally the reactions of disgust, embarrassment, impatience, partisanship, excitement without release, silence without serenity. I say that such things, if I am right about them, are just facts— facts of life, of art now. But it should also be said that they are grammatical facts: they tell us what kind of object a modern work of art is. It asks of us, not exactly *more* in the way of response, but one which is more personal. It promises us, not the re-assembly of community, but personal relationship unsponsored by that community; not the overcoming of our isolation, but the sharing of that isolation—not to save the world out of love, but to save love for the world, until it is responsive again. "Ah, love, let us be true to one another . . . ." We are grateful for the offer, but also appalled by it.

I say "we," and I will be asked "Who?" I will be told that it is not Mr. Arnold speaking to us, but a mask of Arnold speaking to . . . anyway not to us: we don't so much hear his words as overhear them. That explains something. But it does not explain our responsibility in overhearing, in *listening*: nor his in speaking, knowing he's overheard, and meaning to be. What it neglects is that we are to *accept* the words, or refuse them; wish for them, or betray them. What is called for is not merely our interest, nor our transport—these may even serve as betrayals now. What is called for is our acknowledgment that we are implicated, or our rejection of the implication. In dreams begin responsibilities? In listening begins evasion.

Not that it is obvious how intention and sincerity and seriousness are to be established in art, any more than in religion or morality or love. But this is just what I have against the discussions I have read and heard on these topics; they are unreal in their confidence about what establishing an intention, or an attitude, would be like. A man asks me for a candlestick from the mantle and I bring it to him; he looks and says, "No. I meant the other one." Did he? Does his saying this establish his intention? Not in the absence of an understandable continuation. If he simply puts the thing on the floor beside him and I cannot imagine to what point, nor can I imagine what he may want to use it for later, nor can I see what its difference is from the one he rejected, I am not going to say that he *meant* this one rather than the other one. (Perhaps his intention was to demonstrate the completeness of my subservience, obeying pointless requests.) What the continuation will have to be, how it establishes the intention, will vary in range and complexity, with the context.

Take an example from the making of movies, which is relatively free of the ideologies and attitudes we have constructed for the major arts. On my interpretation of *La Strada*, it is a version of the story of Philomel: the Guilietta Massina figure is virtually speechless, she is rudely forced, she tells her change by playing the trumpet, one tune over and over which at the end fills the deserted beach and whose purity at last attacks her barbarous king. Suppose I want to find out whether Fellini intended an allusion to Philomel. If I ask him, and he affirms it, that may end any lingering doubts about its relevance. Suppose he denies it; will I believe him, take his word against my conviction that it is there? In fact, my conviction of the relevance is so strong here that, if I asked Fellini, I would not so much be looking for confirmation of my view as inquiring whether he had recognized this fact about his work. One may ask: "Doesn't this simply prove what those who deny the relevance of intention have always said? What is decisive is what is there, not what the artist intended, or said he intended." What this question proves is that a particular formulation of the problem of intention has been accepted. Because in what I have been urging, this alternative between "what is intended" and "what is there" is just what is being questioned. Intention is no more an efficient cause of an object of art than it is of a human action; in both cases it is a way of understanding the thing done, of describing what happens. "But you admit that Fellini may not have known, or may not find relevant, the connection with Philomel. And if he didn't know, or doesn't see the relevance, surely he *can't* have intended it. And yet it is there, or may be."

What is the relation between what you know (or knew) and what you intend to be doing? It is obvious enough that not everything you know you are doing is something you are intending to be doing (though it will also not be, except in odd circumstances, something you are doing unintentionally either). To take a stock example: you know that firing a gun is making a lot of noise, but only in special circumstances will making the noise be (count as) what it is you are intending to do. But perhaps that is irrelevant: "It is still true that anything you can be said to have intended or to be intending to do is something you know you are doing. Either Fellini did or did not know of the connection with the Philomel story. If he did not know then it follows that he did not intend the connection. If he did know then that connection may or may not have been intended by him. In all these cases, what he knew and what he intended are irrelevant to our response. It is what he has *done* that matters." But it is exactly to find out what someone has done, what he is responsible for, that one investigates his intentions. What does it mean to say "Making the noise was not his intention"? What it comes to is that if asked what he is doing he will not answer (or one will not describe him as) "Making noise." That aspect of what he is doing is obvious, or irrelevant—there is no reason to call attention to it. But suppose there is. There is a child asleep in that house; or terrified by noise; or the noise is a signal of some kind. Suppose he hadn't known. Very well, it can be pointed out to him; and now, should he go on firing the gun, *what* he is doing will be differently described. We might say: his intention will have altered. And yet he would be *doing* the same thing? But the point is: when further relevances of what you are doing, or have done, are pointed out, then you cannot disclaim them by saying that it is not your intention to do those things but only the thing you're concentrating on. "Unintentionally," "inadvertently," "thoughtlessly," etc., would not serve as excuses unless, having needed the excuse, you stop doing the thing that keeps having these unintentional, inadvertent, thoughtless features.

"But doesn't this just show how different the artist's situation is? There isn't going to be some obvious description like 'Firing a gun' to describe what he's done, and even if there were, you couldn't *alter* his intention (whatever that means) by pointing out the further relevances of his work, because in looking for the artist's intention the point surely would not be to get him to stop doing what he is doing, or do something else; his intention is history, forever fixed— whatever it was, it has had *this* result—and the work it has created has consequences only in terms of that work itself. You say that if a man doesn't realize the concomitants of his action you can point them out; but before you point them out they were not known and hence cannot have been a part of *that* intention." The artist's situation is indeed different, but it doesn't follow that what we are interested in, being interested in his work, is not his intention (in the work).

Suppose Fellini hadn't thought of Philomel. How am I to imagine his negative response to my question—when, that is, I find that it doesn't matter what he says? Am I to imagine that he says, "No. I wasn't thinking of that," and there the matter drops? But one would not accept that even in so simple a case as the firing gun: he may not have thought of it before, but he had better think of it now. I am not aesthetically incompetent (any more than I am morally incompetent when I point out that a child is asleep or terrified); I know what kind of consideration is artistically relevant and what is not, as well as anyone else, though I may not be able to articulate this relevance as well as useful critics can, much less create the relevance in a work of art.

I say he had better think about it once I point out the connection; but obviously he may refuse to, and he *can* refuse because this is not a moral context, there is no new practical consequence forthcoming. But there are consequences: if he doesn't see the relevance, I am shaken in my trust in him as an artist. He may not care about that, but I do, and that is all I am concerned with here. Suppose he does acknowledge the relevance, but hadn't thought of it until it was pointed out to him. Wouldn't that in fact just show that he can't have intended it?—So intention cannot be what secures the relevance of one's descriptions of a work.

Now the difference between the artist's case and the simple physical action becomes critical. Everything depends upon how the relevance is, or is not, acknowledged. Suppose he says, "Of course! That's just the feeling I had about my character when I was making the picture. Odd the story never occurred to me." Or: "How ironic. I had tried to translate that story into a modern setting several times with no success. Here, without realizing it, I actually did it." In such cases I am inclined to say that the relevance is intended. (Here, one will have to investigate ordinary cases in which, e.g., dissatisfied with the way you have put something—a phrase, or a vase—you are offered a new alternative and, accepting it, reply: "Yes, that's right. That's what I meant"—when, by hypothesis, *that* alternative had not occurred to you.) At a glance, one might take the second case ("without realizing it") as one of inadvertence rather than intention. But that would be true only if the allusion was one he hadn't wanted, doesn't want now. (In the land he has made, the artist is entitled to everything he wants, if it's there.) Nor am I prompted to add that the intention was *unconscious*. That may well describe certain cases, but its usefulness will have specifically to be made out. What would prompt it here is the idea that intentions must be *conscious*—the same idea which would prompt one to deny that Fellini can have intended the reference if it hadn't occurred to him at the time, if he hadn't been aware of it. But what is the origin of the idea that intentions must be conscious? It is not clear what that means, nor that it means anything at all, apart from a contrast with unconscious intentions; and it is not clear what that means.

Part of its origin is doubtless the fact that you can't be intending to do a thing if you don't *know* you're doing it, or rather don't know how what you are doing could have that consequence (if you didn't know about the child, you can't have intended to frighten it). But what does "knowing it" consist in? Certainly one can know a thing without bearing it in mind (fortunately—otherwise there wouldn't be room for much), or having it occur to you at regular intervals. It makes sense to say Fellini intended (that is to say, Fellini can have intended) the reference to Philomel if he knew the story and now sees its relevance to his own, whether or not the story and its relevance occurred to him at the time. (I do not say that under these conditions he did intend it; knowing is at best necessary, not sufficient for intention. Whether he did intend it depends on what he *did*, on the work itself.) This may still seem puzzling; it may still seem, for example, that no present or future relevation can show what an earlier intention was.

But why is this puzzling? Perhaps it has to do with our, for some reason, not being free to consider what "acknowledging an intention" is, or what "being shown relevance" is. Suppose the man had known about the child but had forgotten. Reminded, he is stunned, and quickly acknowledges his forgetfulness. Without that, or some similar, acknowledgment, the excuse/apology would not be acceptable—would not *be* an excuse or apology. Suppose he has conveniently forgotten; confronted, he may vehemently deny that he had known, or that it matters; or vehemently acknowledge that he had intended to wake or terrify the child. Vehemence here measures the distance between knowing a thing and having to acknowledge it. I imagined Fellini's acknowledgment of the relevance as coming with a sharp recognition, a sense of clarification. Otherwise, it is not an acknowledgment of something he intended or wanted. He might simply have been putting me off.

Perhaps the puzzlement comes from the feeling that it is not enough for him merely to have *known* the story; the knowledge must have been *active* in him, so to speak. And doesn't that mean he must have been aware of it? Two considerations now seem relevant:

(1) It is not necessary for him in fact to have been aware of it; but it is necessary that he can *become* aware of it in a particular way. The man firing the gun can become aware of those further relevances only by being told them, or by further empirical exploration. But the artist becomes aware of them by bethinking himself of them; by, as it were, trying the intention on himself now. This difference is what one would expect. For there is no relevance to point out, in relation to a work of art, which the artist has not himself created. It is he who has put the child there and made it sleep or filled it with fear.

(2) It is, or ought to be, obvious enough that an artist is a man who knows how to *do* something, to make something, that he spends his life trying to learn to do it better, by experience, practice, exercise, perception . . . . And as is familiar with any activity: you can be an expert at it (know how to do it well) without knowing (being aware of) what it is you do exactly; and certainly without being able to say how you do it. (There are obvious problems here. Can you know how to play the clarinet if you can't play the clarinet? You might know how—without being able to—well enough to teach someone to play. Only you won't, as part of your teaching, be able yourself to *demonstrate* the correct way. In certain cases one might wish to say that you couldn't *teach* someone how, but you could *tell* him how.) Suppose someone noticed that Babe Ruth, just before swinging at a pitch, bent his knees in a particular way. Obviously he may not be aware that he does this, but does it follow that it is not done intentionally? If there is reason to believe that bending his knees is an essential part of what makes him good at batting—an explanation of how he does it—I find I want to say that he does it intentionally; he means to. I would not say this about the way he habitually tugs at his cap before gripping the bat, unless it were shown that this was connected with the way he then grips it—e.g., he has some secret substance in the bill of the cap, or it serves to fix his fingers in some special position. Nor would I say this about some action which hindered a performance—the way, for example, one of his team mates drops his shoulder as he swings; he may invariably do this, and be perfectly aware of it, and working hard to get over it: it is unintentional, he doesn't mean to. But all of this is hardly surprising: intending to do something is internally related to wanting something to happen,[7] and discovering an intention is a way of discovering an explanation.

[7] This is one among several points at which acknowledgment is due G. E. M. Anscombe's *Intention*, Oxford and Ithaca, N.Y., 1957, a work which no one involved in this topic will safely neglect.

I

That one is locating intention is what accounts for the fact that a piece of criticism takes the form of an interpretation.

I do not wish to claim that everything we find in a work is something we have to be prepared to say the artist intended to put there. But I am claiming that our not being so prepared is not the inevitable state of affairs; rather, it must be exceptional (at least in successful works of art)—as exceptional as happy accidents, welcome inadvertancies, fortunate mistakes, pure luck.[8] Perhaps the actions of artists produce more such eventualities than other forms of human conduct (hence, the poet as dumb Bard, or wild child, and the function of the Muse). But then they are also fuller of intention (hence, the artist as genius, visionary). Given certain continuations I may want to say: Fellini didn't intend the reference, but, being an artist he did something even better; he re-discovered, or discovered for himself, in himself, the intention of that myth itself, the feelings and wants which originally produced it. Or I may simply say: So it wasn't intentional. I shall be surprised, perhaps led to go over his work again to discover whether I still find the connection as powerful as I did at first; perhaps it is merely a superficial coincidence, and blocks me from a more direct appreciation. But if I do still find it useful, I shall still use it in my reading of the film, not because his intention no longer guides me, but because what it does is exactly guide me (as it guided him). To say that works of art are intentional objects is not to say that each bit of them, as it were, is separately intended; any more than to say a human action is intentional is to say that each physical concomitant of it is separately intended—the noise, that grass crushed where I have stood, that branch broken by the bullet, my sharp intake of breath before the shot, and the eye-blink after . . . . But all these are things I have done, and any may become relevant. In tragedy, consequence altogether outstrips the creature's preview, and nature and society exact their price for a manageable world; in comedy, the price is born by nature and society themselves, smiling upon their creatures. In morality, our interest in intention,

---

[8] The "must" in "must be exceptional" is a point of Transcendental Logic. It doesn't mean: Invariably, most of what is in the object is intended. It means: Our concept of a work of art is such that what is not intended in it has to be thought of, or explained, in contrast to intention, at the same level as intention, as the qualification of a human action. Of course not every portion of an interpretation will be directed simply to pointing out something which is there, i.e., something the artist may or may not have intended. Sometimes it will be directed toward helping us appreciate what has been pointed out. Sometimes this will involve evaluating the intention—e.g., as cheap, childish, courageous, perverse, willful; sometimes it will involve evaluating its execution, as, e.g., crude, brutal, thoughtless, inattentive; sometimes it will involve comparing the given work with another one whose intentions are different.

given the need to confront someone's conduct, is to localize his responsibility within the shift of events. In art, our interest in intention, given the fact that we are confronted by someone's work, is to locate ourselves in its shift of events. In all cases, the need is for coming to terms, for taking up the import of a human gesture. In all, I may use terms to describe what someone has done which he himself would not use, or may not know. (Here the problem of oblique contexts is explicitly relevant.) Whether what I say he has done is just or not just is something that will require justification, by further penetration into what has happened, what is there. What counts is what is *there*, says the philosopher who distrusts appeals to intention. Yes, but everything that is there is something a man has *done*.

Games are places where intention does not count, human activities in which intention need not generally be taken into account; because in games *what happens* is described solely in terms set by the game itself, because the consequences one is responsible for are limited *a priori* by the rules of the game. In morality, tracing an intention limits a man's responsibility; in art, it dilates it completely. The artist is responsible for everything that happens in his work—and not just in the sense that it is done, but in the sense that it is *meant*. It is a terrible responsibility; very few men have the gift and the patience and the singleness to shoulder it. But it is all the more terrible, when it *is* shouldered, not to appreciate it, to refuse to understand something meant so well.

I break off with one further way in which questioning the artist may work itself out. Instead of considering my inquiries with due solemnity, he may tell me to mind my business, or my manners; or deliberately mislead me. (So may his work. And of course by now the artist has dropped out anyway; it is his work we are interviewing.) What would this signify? Perhaps that he has said all he can, conveyed his intentions as fully as his powers allow, in the work itself—as if to say: "You want to spare yourself the difficulty of understanding me, but there is no way else to understand me; otherwise it would not have cost me such difficulty to make myself exactly understood." One might have been aware of that oneself, and not meant to be getting out of difficulty, but asking help to get in further. Why, in those circumstances, would the artist turn away? In *those* circumstances he might not. But then claiming to be in those circumstances is a large claim, and how does one justify it? Asking anyone about his intentions is asking whether he is meeting his responsibilities, asking an explanation of his conduct. And what gives one the right? In morality the right is given in one's relation to what has been done, or to the man who has done it. In art, it has to be earned, through the talent of understanding, the skill of commitment, and truthfulness to one's response—the ways the artist earned his initial right to our attention. If we have earned the right to question it, the object itself will answer; otherwise not. There is poetic justice.

MYSTICAL EXPERIENCE*

NINIAN SMART

Unfortunately the term 'mysticism' and its relations ('mystical,' etc.) are used by different people in different senses. For the purposes of this paper I shall treat mysticism as primarily consisting in an interior or introvertive quest, culminating in certain interior experiences which are not described in terms of sense experience or of corresponding mental images, etc. But such an account needs supplementation in two directions: first, examples of people who typify the mystical life should be given, and second, mysticism should be distinguished from that which is *not* (on this usage) mysticism.

First, I would propose that the following folk typify the mystical life: St. John of the Cross, Tauler, Eckhart, al-Hallāj, Shankara, the Buddha, Lao-Tzu (if he existed!), and many yogis.

Second, mysticism is *not* prophetism, and can be distinguished from devotionalism or *bhakti* religion (though mysticism often mingles with these forms of religious life and experience). I would propose that the following are *not* mystics in the relevant sense in which the Buddha and the others *are* mystics: Isaiah, Jeremiah, Muhammad, Nichiren, Calvin, Rāmānuja, and Wesley.

Needless to say, such expressions as 'the mystical body of Christ' have no necessary connection with mysticism in the proposed sense. It is unfortunate that a word originally referring to a certain sort of dramatic ritual and by extension to sacramentalism has come to be used in a different sense. Since, however, 'mysticism' is now most often used to refer to the mode of life and experience typified by men like St. John of the Cross and the Buddha, I shall use the term, though 'contemplation' and 'contemplative' can be less misleading.

Thus 'mysticism' here will be used to refer to the contemplative life and experience, as distinguished from prophetism, devotionalism, and sacramentalism (though we must bear in mind the fact mentioned above, that other forms of religious life are often interwoven with mysticism).

In a number of works Professor R. C. Zaehner has distinguished between three categories of mystical experience: (1) panenhenic or nature mysticism (exemplified by Rimbaud, Jefferies, and others);

* I am grateful to Professor H. D. Lewis for allowing me to use substantial portions of an article "Interpretation and Mystical Experience," which I contributed to *Religious Studies*, I, 1965, pp. 75-87.

(2) monistic mysticism (as found in Advaita, Sāṁkhya-Yoga, etc.);
(3) theistic mysticism (as in the Christian tradition, the *Gītā*, etc.).

His distinction between (1) and the other two is correct and valuable. The sense of rapport with nature often comes to people in a striking and intimate way; but it is to be contrasted with the interior, and properly speaking mystical, experience in which a man, as it were, plumbs the depths of his own soul. It is probable that Zen *satori* is to be equated with the panenhenic experience, though Zen also makes use of the general pattern of Buddhist yoga which elsewhere culminates in an interior rather than a panenhenic type of experience.

But is Zaehner's distinction between (2) and (3) a valid one? He criticizes those who believe that mysticism is everywhere the same— a belief sometimes held in conjunction with the neo-Vedantin thesis that behind the various forms of religion there is a higher truth realizable in contemplative experience and best expressed through the doctrine of a universal Self (or Ātman). On Zaehner's view, monistic mysticism is "realising the eternal oneness of one's own soul" as contrasted with the "mysticism of the love of God."[1] The latter attainment is typical of Christian, Muslim, and other theistic contemplation.

But does the difference lie in the experiences themselves? The concepts *God* and *Self* belong to diverse theologies, and it may be that roughly the same experience is interpreted differently in accordance with these theologies. We need to examine in more detail the methodology of the evaluation and interpretation of mystical experience.

That some distinction must be made between interpretation and experience is clear. For it is generally recognized, and certainly by Zaehner, that there are types of experience cutting across different religions and theologies; that is, it is recognized that the mystic of one religion and the mystic of another faith can have what is substantially the same experience. Thus both Christian and Muslim mystics come under Zaehner's category of theistic mysticism, while, for him, Advaitin and Yogin mysticism belong to the same category. But the interpretations within a type differ. Thus the Yogin believes in a plurality of eternal *purushas* but not in a single Ātman. Consequently the Yogin account of liberation, and therefore of contemplative experience, differs from that of Advaita. Thus on Zaehner's own thesis it becomes very necessary to distinguish between experience and interpretation, when two experiences belong to the same class but have rather diverse modes of interpretation.

[1] R. C. Zaehner, *At Sundry Times*, London, 1958, p. 132.

Nevertheless, the distinction between experience and interpretation is not clear-cut. The reason for this is that the concepts used in describing and explaining an experience differ in their degree of *ramification*. That is, where a concept occurs as part of a doctrinal scheme it gains its meaning in part from a range of doctrinal statements taken to be true. For example, the term 'God' in the Christian context gains part of its characteristic meaning from such statements as "God created the world," "Jesus Christ is God," "God has acted in history," etc.

Thus when Suso writes "In this merging of itself in God the spirit passes away," he is describing the contemplative experience by means of the highly ramified concept *God*, the less ramified concept *spirit*, and the still less ramified concept *pass away*. To understand the statement it is necessary to bear in mind the doctrinal ramifications contained in it. Thus it follows, for Suso as a Christian, that in this merging of itself the spirit is merged in the Creator of the world, the Father of Our Lord Jesus Christ, etc.

By contrast, the degree of ramification in some descriptions is very low. For instance "When the spirit by the loss of its self-consciousness has in very truth established its abode in this glorious and dazzling obscurity": here something of the nature of the experience is conveyed without any doctrine's being presupposed as true (except in so far as the concept *spirit* may involve some belief in an eternal element within man). This, then, is a relatively unramified description. Thus descriptions of mystical experience range from the highly ramified to those which have a very low degree of ramification.[2]

It is to be noted that ramifications may enter into the descriptions either because of the intentional nature of the experience or because of reflection upon it. Thus a person brought up in a Christian environment and strenuously practising the Christian life may have a contemplative experience which he *sees* as union with God. The whole spirit of the interior quest will affect the way he sees his experience; or, to put it another way, the whole spirit of his quest will enter into his experience. On the other hand, a person might only come to see his experience in this way after the event, as it were: upon reflection he interprets his experience in theological categories.

In all descriptions of mystical experience, then, we ought to be on the lookout for ramifications. Their degree can be crudely estimated by asking: How many propositions are presupposed as true by the description in question?

It would also seem to follow, if we bear in mind the notion of

[2] See my "Mystical Experience" in *Sophia*, I, 1962, pp. 19ff.

ramification, that the higher the degree, the less is the description guaranteed by the experience itself. For where there is a high degree of ramification, some statements will be presupposed which rest on grounds other than those of immediate mystical experience. Thus a mystic who claims to become united with Christ presupposes that the historical Jesus is the Christ; and the historicity of Jesus is guaranteed by the written records, not by an interior experience. Again, where contemplation is regarded as a means of liberation from rebirth, the description of the mystical experience may involve reference to this doctrine (thus the concept *nirvāna* presupposes the truth of the rebirth doctrine): to say that someone has in this life attained the peace and insight of nirvāna is also to claim that he will not be reborn. But the truth of the rebirth doctrine is not discovered by mystical experience as such. It is true that the Buddhist yogin may claim supernormal knowledge of previous lives. But this is in the nature of memory, if anything, and is to be distinguished from the formless, imageless inner experience which accrues upon the practice of *jhāna*. Also, Buddhists appeal to other empirical evidence and philosophical arguments in support of the claim that the rebirth doctrine is true.[3]

A further methodological point is also important. Descriptions, etc., of religious experience may be made from various points of view. There is the description given by the man himself, in terms of his own tradition. There is the description which others of his own tradition may give. Also, men of another tradition may describe his experience in terms of *their* tradition or standpoint. Thus if a Christian says that the Buddha's Enlightenment-experience involved some kind of interior vision of God, he is describing the experience from his own point of view and not from that of the Buddha. Crucially, then, we should distinguish between a mystic's interpretation of his own experience and the interpretation which may be placed upon it from a different point of view. We must distinguish between what may be called *auto*-interpretation and *hetero*-interpretation.

The difference between the two will depend on, first, the degree of ramification involved and, second, the divergence between the presupposed truths incorporated in the ramification. For example, the Christian evaluation of the Buddha's Enlightenment-experience described above uses the concept *God* in the Christian (or at least the theistic) sense. The Buddhist description on the other hand does not. Thus the Christian hetero-interpretation presupposes that God created the world, a proposition not accepted in the Buddhist auto-interpretation. By contrast the Jewish and Christian interpre-

---

[3] See my *Doctrine and Argument in Indian Philosophy*, London, 1964, ch. XII.

tations of Isaiah's experience in the Temple overlap in great measure. This is because the beliefs presupposed coincide over quite a wide range.

These methodological observations, though rather obvious, need stating because they are too commonly neglected.

We may conclude, so far, that a description of a mystical experience can fall under one of the following heads:

(a) Auto-interpretation with a low degree of ramification (or for short: low auto-interpretation);
(b) Hetero-interpretation with a low degree of ramification (low hetero-interpretation);
(c) Auto-interpretation with a high degree of ramification (high auto-interpretation);
(d) Hetero-interpretation with a high degree of ramification (high hetero-interpretation).

A high hetero-interpretation of experience *E* will usually imply the falsity or inadequacy of a high auto-interpretation of *E*, and conversely. It would therefore seem to be a sound principle to try to seek a low hetero-interpretation coinciding well with a low auto-interpretation. In this way an agreed phenomenological account of *E* will be arrived at. But since *E* will often be affected by its high auto-interpretation, it is also important to understand this auto-interpretation, without obscuring it by means of a high hetero-interpretation.

I shall argue that Zaehner's distinction between monistic and theistic mysticism partly depends on his own high hetero-interpretation, and partly on his not distinguishing between high and low auto-interpretation.

A difficulty about Zaehner's classification arises once we examine Buddhism. It is undoubtedly the case that Buddhism—and very clearly Theravāda Buddhism—centers on mystical experience. The Eightfold Path incorporates and culminates in a form of yoga which may bring the peace and insight of nirvāna to the saint. Crucial in this yoga is the practice of the *jhānas* or stages of meditation. It is thus necessary for any account of mysticism to take Buddhist experience and tradition seriously. But regrettably (from Zaehner's point of view) Buddhism denies the soul or eternal self. Zaehner, in order to fit Buddhism into the monistic pigeonhole, denies the denial, and ascribes an *ātman* doctrine to the Buddha.

This will not do, for a number of reasons, which can be rehearsed very briefly.[4] First, even if the Buddha did teach an *ātman*, we

[4] A fuller criticism is to be found in my *Doctrine and Argument in Indian Philosophy*, pp. 211 ff.

still have to reckon with the Buddhists. The phenomenon of Buddhist mysticism, not involving an *ātman*-type auto-interpretation remains a widespread and important feature of man's religious history. Second, it is asking a lot to make us believe that a doctrine which has been eschewed by nearly all Buddhists (with the possible exception of the *pudgalavādins*, who significantly did not dare use the term '*ātman*,' though their Buddhist opponents castigated them for wanting to introduce the idea) was explicitly taught by the Buddha. Third, it is easy enough to play around with the texts by translating '*atta*' with a capital, as "Self." Thus Zaehner translates '*attagarahī*' as "that which the Self would blame,"[5] and so on. The word '*ātta*' is very common and has an ordinary usage, which gives much scope for soulful translation. Fourth, the Buddha himself is reported to have asserted that though it is wrong to identify the self with the body, it is better for the uninstructed man to make this mistake than to commit the opposite error of believing in an eternal soul.[6] Consequently, Zaehner cannot well rely on the passages "illustrating what the Self is not"[7]—it is not the body, feelings, dispositions, etc. Their import is clearly explained by the Hume-like analysis found in the famous passage of the *Milinda-pañha* (40-45). For these and other reasons, Zaehner's interpretation cannot seriously be defended.

But embarrassing consequences flow from this conclusion. It means that a main form of mysticism does not involve the monistic auto-interpretation.

Nevertheless, Zaehner could still argue as follows. Admittedly a monistic auto-interpretation is not present among Buddhist contemplatives: but it is still reasonable to hetero-interpret their attainment in a monistic fashion. We can still say that what the Buddhist *really* achieves in and through contemplation is the isolation of eternal soul.

Such a defense, however, implies that there can be a misunderstanding on the part of a mystic as to what it is he is attaining. It implies that auto-interpretations can be widely mistaken, in so far as they are ramified. Likewise, since Zaehner classifies both Yoga and Advaita together as monistic, and since their doctrinal auto-interpretations differ very widely, within the Hindu context it has to be admitted that wrong auto-interpretations can occur.

Let us bring this out more explicitly. According to Zaehner, Buddhist, Yoga, and Advaitin mystics belong together, and fit into the same monistic category; and yet the following three doctrines of liberation are propounded by them:

[5] *Sutta-nipata*, 788. See *At Sundry Times*, pp. 98-101.
[6] *Saṁyutta-nikāya*, ii, 95.
[7] *At Sundry Times*, p. 101.

(1) That there are no eternal selves, but only impermanent individuals who are, however, capable of liberation, through attaining nirvāna in this life, in which case they will no longer be reborn.

(2) That there is an infinite number of eternal selves, who through Yoga can attain isolation or liberation, a state in which the soul exists by itself, no longer implicated in nature and in the round of rebirth.

(3) That there is but one Self, which individuals can realize, and which is identical with Brahman as the ground of being (which at a lower level of truth manifests itself as a personal Lord and Creator)—such a realization bringing about a cessation of the otherwise continuously reborn individual.

Now these are obviously very diverse doctrines. Why should the crucial difference lie between them and theism? Is not the difference between (2) and (3) equally striking? If the monistic category includes heterogeneous high auto-interpretations, there is no guarantee that we should not place *all* mystics, including theists, in the same category—and then explain the differences between them not in terms of so many radically diverse experiences, but in terms of varied auto-interpretation. The gaps within the monistic category are big enough for it not to seem implausible to count the gap between monism and theism as no wider.

Admit that high auto-interpretations can be mistaken, and there is no great reason to isolate theistic mysticism as belonging to a separate category.

If I am right in proposing this on methodological grounds, we can go on to explain the difference between Yoga (say) and theism by reference to what goes on outside the context of the mystical life. The devotional and prophetic experiences of a personal God—prophetism and *bhakti* religion—help to explain why the theist sees his contemplative experience in a special way. He already considers that there is evidence of a personal Lord and Creator: in the silent brightness of inner contemplative ecstasy it is natural (or supernatural) to identify what is found within with the Lord who is worshipped without.[8] *A priori*, then, there is no special call to assign theistic mysticism to a special pigeon hole. Of course, there are theological motives for trying to do this. It avoids some ticklish questions, and it suggests that there is something very special about theistic mysticism. It is a covert means of preaching theism. Now doubtless theism should be preached, but *fairly*. Methodologically, the assignment of theism to a speical pigeon hole is suspect. The arguments are more complex and difficult than we think.

[8] See *Doctrine and Argument in Indian Philosophy*, Ch. X, where an analysis along these lines is worked out in some detail.

But it may be replied to all this that the discussion has been largely *a priori*. Do we not have to look at the actual words of theistic mystics? Of course. But I shall content myself with examining some passages which Zaehner quotes in favor of his own position.

An important part of his argument rests on a couple of passages from Ruysbroeck. I quote from these.

> Now observe that whenever man is empty and undistracted in his senses by images, and free and unoccupied in his highest powers, he attains rest by purely natural means. And all men can find and possess this rest in themselves by their mere nature, without the grace of God, if they are able to empty themselves of sensual images and of all action.[9]

Zaehner comments that Ruysbroeck has in effect described (Advaita) Vedāntin mysticism. Talking of men who have obtained this "natural rest," Ruysbroeck goes on:

> Through the natural rest, which they feel and have in themselves in emptiness, they maintain that they are free, and united with God, without mean, and that they are advanced beyond all the exercises of the Holy Church, and beyond the commandments of God, and beyond the law, and beyond all the virtuous works which one can in any way practise.[10]

Now it will be noted that Ruysbroeck's criticism rests chiefly on moral grounds. He condemns quietists for arrogance, complacency, and ethical sterility. They do not properly connect their inner experience with the God taught by the Church, who makes demands upon men, and who wishes that they may love him. But the ordinances and teachings of the Church do not spring from mystical experience: they have other sources. And moral insights are not simply derived from contemplation. In short, the criteria for judging mystical experience are (here) partly exterior to the contemplative life. Thus, even given that Ruysbroeck is a good guide in these matters, and this need not be so, we might still say: The trouble with monistic quietists is a failure in their interpretation of their experience—they do not really see the God of the Bible and of the Church there. But this does not at all entail that, given a low interpretation, these experiences differ radically for those of theistic mystics.

Quietists, for Ruysbroeck, are not sufficiently aware of the working of God's grace. But the doctrine of grace (and by contrast, nature) is a theological account of God's activity. A person could

[9] R. C. Zaehner, *Mysticism Sacred and Profane*, Oxford, 1957, p. 170.
[10] *Ibid.*, p. 171.

have a genuine mystical experience, but be wrong in not ascribing it to God's grace. Ruysbroeck's high hetero-interpretation of monistic quietism conflicts with the latter's high auto-interpretation. But the experiences for all that could belong to the same type. In short, the Ruysbroeck passages are quite compatible with my thesis, and do not strongly support the Zaehner analysis.

Zaehner also makes use of a very interesting passage from al-Ghazāli, part of which reads as follows:

> The mystics, after their ascent to the heavens of Reality, agree that they saw nothing in existence except God the One. Some of them attained this state through discursive reasoning, others reached it by savouring and experiencing it. From these all plurality entirely fell away. They were drowned in pure solitude: their reason was lost in it, and they became as if dazed in it. They no longer had the capacity to recollect aught but God, nor could they in any wise remember themselves. Nothing was left to them but God. They became drunk with a drunkenness in which their reason collapsed. One of them said "I am God (the Truth)." Another said "Glory be to me, How great is my glory," while another said "Within my robe is naught but God." But the words of lovers when in a state of drunkenness must be hidden away and not broadcast. However, when their drunkenness abates and the sovereignty of their reason is restored,—and reason is God's scale upon earth,—they know that this was not actual identity .... For it is not impossible that a man should be confronted by a mirror and should look into it, and not see the mirror at all, and that he should think that the form he saw in the mirror was the form of the mirror itself and identical with it . . . [11]

What Ghazāli is saying here (to translate into my own jargon) is that the mystic's auto-interpretation of the experience as involving actual identity with God is mistaken, and that the correct interpretation must say that there is some distinction between the soul and God. In the passage quoted he goes on to explain how the mystic, in his self-naughting, is not conscious of himself, and this is a main reason for the language of identity.

This seems to be a clear indication that the monistic and theistic experiences are essentially similar; and that it is the correct *interpretation* of them which is at issue. The theist must maintain, in order to make sense of worship and devotion, that there is a distinction between the human individual and God. The non-theist, not being so much concerned with devotion (though he may find a place for it, at the popular level), can more happily speak of identity with

[11] *Ibid.*, pp. 157-158.

ultimate Reality, or can even dispense (as in Theravāda Buddhism) with anything to be identical *with*. Thus the question of the best interpretation of mystical experience turns, at least partly, on whether devotion and worship are important. Or more generally: the question of interpretation is the same as the question of God. One cannot answer this by reference to auto-interpretations of mystical experience alone; for they conflict, and they have ramifications extending beyond the sphere of such experience itself.

This is why my thesis does not at all entail that proponents of neo-Vedāntin views of a "perennial philosophy," involving a doctrine of the Absolute Self,[12] are right. The thesis "All introvertive mysticism is, as experience, essentially the same" does not entail any doctrine. Truth of doctrine depends mainly on other considerations, and this is true of the doctrine of the Absolute Self.

I have tried to argue that the interpretation of mystical experience depends at least in part on evidence, etc., not given in the experience itself; and that it is therefore always important to ask about the degree to which non-experiential data are incorporated into descriptions of mystical experience. Watch the ramifications! I can best illustrate this point by a passage written by Zaehner himself:

> We have already said that when the mystic claims attributes that are necessarily divine and demonstrably not human,—such as omnipotence and omniscience,—it is fairly clear that he is not enjoying union with God, but rather some sort of natural mystical experience. Apart from this important consideration it would seem that the mystic who is genuinely inspired by the divine love, will show this to the world by the holiness of his life and by an abiding humility in face of the immense favors bestowed which he always will see to be God's doing, not his own. Only such criteria can enable us to distinguish between the genuine state of union with God and the "natural" or rather "praeternatural" phenomena we have been discussing.[13]

The two criteria here mentioned can be called respectively the theological and the moral. The theological criterion shows, or is claimed to show, that the mystic cannot have enjoyed real union with God because he makes false theological claims on his own behalf. The moral criterion can show that a mystic has not enjoyed real union with God because his life is not holy, or not humble. Some comments are in order.

First, both criteria are indirect. If they are, as Zaehner here

[12] See, for instance, W. T. Stace, *Mysticism and Philosophy*, Philadelphia and New York, 1960, which comes to this conclusion.

[13] *Mysticism Sacred and Profane, op. cit.*, p. 193.

says, the *only* criteria that distinguish genuine union with God from something else, then one cannot establish this latter discrimination on the basis of a phenomenological account of the experience itself, but rather on the basis of the verbal and other behavior of the contemplative. This supports my thesis.

Second, the first criterion depends on the truth of theism. This is why the interpretation and evaluation of mystical experience from a doctrinal point of view cannot be separated from the truth of theism. The criterion could not work for a Vedāntin.

Third, to some extent the same is true of the moral criterion. For humility is a virtue for the theist, who sees wonder and holiness in the Divine Being; but it need not be a virtue for the non-theist. In so far as moral ideas depend on theology (and they do in part) one cannot really separate the moral from the theological criterion.

The above arguments by themselves do not establish the truth of my thesis that monistic and theistic contemplative experiences are (except in so far as they are affected by auto-interpretations) essentially the same. But I hope that they are sufficient to cast doubt on the Zaehner analysis.

Mysticism is not the same as prophetism and *bhakti* religion; but it may gain its auto-interpretations from these latter types of religion. But there is no need to take all interpretations as phenomenological descriptions, and this is the main point of this paper. To put the possibility which I am canvassing in a simple form, it can be reduced to the following theses:

(1) Phenomenologically mysticism is everywhere the same.

(2) Different flavors, however, accrue to the experiences of the mystics because of their ways of life and modes of auto-interpretation.

(3) The truth of an interpretation depends in large measure on factors extrinsic to the mystical experience itself.

Thus the question of whether mysticism is a valid means of knowledge concerning the Transcendent is only part of a much wider set of theological questions.

Finally, let me express my debt to Zaehner's learning and fertility of ideas. If I have criticized a main thesis of his, it is because it is itself an important contribution to the discussion of mysticism. In my view, his analysis is wrong; but interestingly false propositions are worth far more than a whole lot of boringly true ones.

COMMENTS

NELSON PIKE

I

Consider two pictures and two descriptions of these pictures:

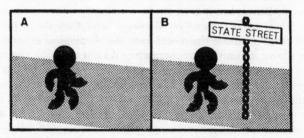

A. Man walking on street.   B. Man walking on State Street.

As regards the first picture, Description A mentions nothing more than is given in the picture. It could be verified by reference to the content of the picture alone. The same cannot be said of Description B. If Smith were to describe the first picture as "Man walking on State Street," we would expect him to go on to tell us how he knows it is *State* Street. This is not an item given in the picture. It is not one of the "pictured-facts." Smith might justify his description as follows: I know that the picture was painted by Green. And Green told me that he intended it to be of Jones walking on State Street. In this case, the justification of the description (whether adequate or not) draws on knowledge gained from some source other than the picture itself. Beliefs about the intentions of the artist are built into the description of the picture's content.

However, the case is not the same with respect to the second picture. Here, the picture includes a sign bearing the name 'State Street.' Thus either of the given descriptions might be used to describe the "pictured-facts." The picture pictures a man walking on a street; or (more specifically) the picture pictures a man walking on State Street. The justification of either of these descriptions would involve reference to nothing beyond the explicit content of the picture itself.

One more note on this topic: The form of words used to talk about the content of pictures need not commit one to the existence of something other than the picture. If one says of a picture that it is "Of a man walking on State Street," one need not affirm that there is (or was) some particular man (Jones) whom the picture is of; or that there is (or was) some particular street (State Street) upon which he walked. As long as the description of the picture mentions only the "pictured-facts" (i.e., as a straightforward report of what is actually given in the picture), the description need not carry ontological import. My son has a picture of Paul Bunyan riding his blue ox Babe.

II

In the *Brihadaranyaka Upanishad*, Yagnavalkya speaks as follows:

As long as there is duality, one sees *the other*, one hears *the other*, one smells *the other*, one speaks to *the other*, one thinks of *the other*, one knows *the other*; but when for the illuminated soul the all is dissolved in the Self, who is there to be seen by whom, who is there to be smelt by whom, who is there to be heard by whom, who is there to be spoken to by whom, who is there to be taught by whom, who is there to be known by whom? Ah Maitreyi, my beloved, the Intelligence which reveals all—by what shall it be revealed? By whom shall the knower be known? The Self is described as *not this, not that*. It is incomprehensible, for it cannot be comprehended; undecaying, for it never decays; unattached, for it never attaches itself; unbounded for it is never bound. By whom, of my beloved shall the knower be known?[1]

If we can take this passage as a description of the mystical experience (i.e., the Self in its "illuminated" state), it would seem that the author intends us to understand the experience as one in which one becomes aware of himself as an "undifferentiated unity" (W. T. Stace's phrase). One is not aware of *another*. The *self* as a "not this—not that" is the sole content of the experience. It is the only "thing" of which one is aware.

Let us now suppose that I describe Yagnavalkya's experience as one in which one is aware of oneself related in some way (perhaps *united*) with God. This would be to offer what Mr. Smart calls a "ramified" description of the experience. I would be describing the experience in terms of my own doctrinal beliefs. Yagnavalkya explicitly says that (phenomenologically) the experience is not of-another. If I claim that the experience is one in which one is aware of self when the Self is in some special relation to something else

[1] *The Upanishad: Breath of the Eternal*, tr. Swami Prabhavananda and Frederick Manchester, New York, 1957, pp. 67-68.

K

(viz. God), my description cannot be understood as a purely phenomenological account of the content of the experience. It would be like Description B of the *first* picture of Jones walking on the street. It incorporates theological convictions gained from sources other than the actual content of the experience being described.

Now consider the following report cited by William James in the third chapter of *Varieties of Religious Experience*.

> There was not a mere consciousness of something there, but fused in the central happiness of it, a startling awareness of some ineffable good. Not vague either, not like the emotional effect of some poem, or scene or blossom, of music, but the sure knowledge of the close presence of a sort of mighty person, and after it went, the memory persisted as the one perception of reality. Everything else might be a dream, but not that.[2]

In this passage, the reporter seems clearly to be saying that his religious experience was one in which he was aware of himself in the presence of someone other than himself—some other person who was good and mighty. That he was in contact with *another* seems to be one of the "pictured-facts." The experience was (phenomenologically) of-*another*.

Let us now suppose (as we did above) that I describe this experience as one in which the reporter was aware of Self in contact with God. This could well be a way of describing just the phenomenological content of the experience. I might simply be reporting that he experienced himself in contact with an ineffably good and overwhelmingly powerful person. In this case, my description would be similar to Description B of the *second* picture of Jones walking on the Street. Just as State Street was explicitly pictured in the second picture, so God is explicitly experienced in this second experience. Thus, just as the description of the picture, "Man walking on *State* Street," mentions nothing other than the pictured-facts, so the description of the experience as "self in contact with God" mentions nothing other than the explicit content of the experience.

I have three notes to add to this point:

Firstly, let us suppose that the reporter whose experience we have just discussed was a Christian believer. Let us suppose that he was a committed Christian prior to his experience. One might hold that the fact that he experienced himself in contact with a good and mighty person was in some way determined by his prior theological beliefs. Had he not believed in the existence of God, he would not

[2] New York, Modern Library ed., 1902, p. 60. Cf. also the report given by James on p. 66.

have experienced himself in contact with such a person. Let us grant this. The description of the experience as "Self in contact with God" would still be a purely phenomenological description. Prior to his dream, my son believed that Paul Bunyan's ox was blue. As a consequence, he dreamed of himself riding on a *blue* ox. But that the dream-ox was experienced as *blue* is part of the phenomenological description of the dream. It is not an item my son incorporated into the description of the dream after waking, as a consequence of his belief that the ox was blue.

Secondly, in describing the reporter's experience as "self in contact with God" we do not commit ourselves to the existence of some ineffably good and all powerful being, God. The reporter himself might describe his experience as one in which he experienced himself in contact with God and then go on to *deny* the existence of God. This would be to acknowledge the experience as hallucinatory. Though this is not what usually happens (as is evident in the passage quoted), still there would be no conceptual difficulty in such an admission. As long as the description is offered as a purely phenomenological account of the content of the experience, it involves no ontological commitment on the part of the one offering the description.

Thirdly, James's reporter tells us that he was aware of a good and mighty person. By what marks did he determine that what he was aware of was a person, or (given that he was aware of a person) that the person in question was good and mighty? For example, did the experience involve a visual image of a man having a kindly face and big muscles? If it did, then we know why he says that he was aware to a person who was good and mighty. Of course, James's reporter would probably reject this suggestion. He would probably say that his experience involved no (visual) *image* whatsoever. Then how did he know that he experienced a good and mighty person? I think this line of questioning is misguided. Suppose I report a dream in which I was riding a carousel and the President of the United States was riding the horse beside me. By what mark did I determine that there was a person riding beside me; or (given that I experienced a person riding beside me) that the person in question was the President of the United States? I might well have no answer to this question. I might go on to say that in my dream I was so nervous about this frolic with the President that I could not bring myself to look at him. I had no visual image of a person bearing certain presidential features. I had no visual image of a person at all. That I was aware of the President riding beside me was an immediate datum of the dream. I do not need to itemize criteria by which I determined the content of my experience. So too in the case of James's reporter. One can be aware of himself in the presence of a good and mighty person without being aware of the identifying marks by which good and powerful persons are ordinarily recognized.[3]

III

I should now like to consider a passage from Chapter XI of Jan von Ruysbroeck's *The Adornment of the Spiritual Marriage*:

> And the bare, uplifted memory feels itself enwrapped and established in an abysmal Absence of Image. And thereby the created image is united above reason in a threefold way with its Eternal Image, which is the origin of its being and its life; and this origin is preserved and possessed, essentially and eternally, through a simple seeing in an imageless void; and so a man is lifted up above reason in a threefold manner into the Unity, and in a onefold manner into the Trinity. Yet the creature does not become God, for the union takes place in God through grace and our homeward-turning love: and therefore the creature in its inward contemplation feels a distinction and an otherness between itself and God . . . .
>
> There (in the mystical experience) all is full and overflowing, for the spirit feels itself to be one truth and one richness and one unit with God. Yet even here there is an essential tending toward, and therein is an essential distinction between the being of the soul and the Being of God; and this is the highest and finest distinction which we are able to feel.[4]

There is a good deal in this passage which is hard to grasp. But one point seems to emerge with some clarity—viz. that while in the mystical experience one "feels" himself "lifted up into a unity" with God, one is constantly aware of the distinction between himself and God. In von Ruysbroeck's words, the soul "feels" a "distinction and an otherness between itself and God"—"[one feels] an essential distinction between the being of the soul and the Being of God." The point seems to be that in the mystical experience one is aware of ("feels") the self in contact with another. That the other is *another* is part of the content of the experience. It is one of the "pictured-facts."

This brings me to a direct comment on the central thesis of Mr. Smart's paper.

---

[3] The point made in this paragraph was introduced into the discussion at Oberlin by Richard Hensen.

[4] Tr. C. A. Wynschenck Dom., London, 1916, pp. 243-244.

R. C. Zaehner has divided mystical experiences into "monistic" and "theistic" types. In the first, the mystic is aware only of self. He is aware of self as an "undifferentiated unity." Yagnavalkya's experience was of this type. In the theistic experience the mystic experiences himself in contact with (or united with) another—viz. God. Mr. Smart has argued that this distinction is not warranted. Those who describe their experiences as "self in contact with God" may well have had the same experience (phenomenologically) as those who describe it as "self as an undifferentied unity." In the former case, extra-experiential theological beliefs have been incorporated into the description of the experience. The truth of such descriptions thus depends not on the actual content of the experience itself, but on the truth of theism considered as a metaphysical doctrine. It may well be that in the mystical experience, the self *is* in contact with God. But to say that it is, is not to describe the content of the experience. It is to affirm a connection between the self and some metaphysical entity (God) and thus to commit oneself to the existence of that entity.

I am inclined to think that Mr. Smart may be right in a large number of cases. It might well be that in describing mystical experiences as "self in contact with God" scholars of mysticism (such as Mr. Zaehner) and mystics themselves are often providing theological interpretations of the experiences and are not confining themselves to pure phenomenological accounts of the content of the experiences. But I am also inclined to think that as regards von Ruysbroeck's mystical experience this thesis cannot be sustained. Here, as in the report taken from William James, the description of the experience as "self in contact with God" (or at least "self in contact with *another*") appears to be a purely phenomenological account whose truth depends not at all on the truth of theism. One would have to discount an item explicitly given in the phenomenological (not the theological) account of von Ruysbroeck's experience in order to crowd him into the same class with Yagnavalkya. As to how many other classical mystics should be classified along with von Ruysbroeck (instead of Yagnavalkya) I shall not attempt to say. This question could be settled only by a careful examination of their actual reports. And in a large number of cases (I dare say) the texts will be such as to permit no firm conclusion on the issue.

What then shall we say about Zaehner's distinction between monistic and theistic mystical experiences? I think we must admit that the distinction is warranted. We can find instances of both types. But, of course, whether Zaehner's distinction provides a useful and interesting basis for dividing up the class of mystical experiences is still an open question. I should think a decision on this last point would depend to some extent on how frequently experiences of the theistic variety crop up in the history of mysticism. The question of frequency (as I have just said) is one I have not tried to answer and one which I suspect would be very difficult to settle.

COMMENTS

PAUL F. SCHMIDT

When a mystic communicates with us about his mystical experience or insight, he will do so with a language that involves one or more conceptual systems. Such conceptual systems are so deeply imbedded in a language that we can easily overlook the extent to which they link us with some particular conception of knowledge and reality. My basic criticism of Smart's paper is his failure to notice the extent to which his own and Zaehner's views concerning one or more types of mysticism are influenced by different conceptual systems. When we put what each claims within the context of its conceptual system, we can understand their disagreements as well as what each has left out. To do this, I offer the following model which deliberately simplifies a very complex situation in order to bring into focus some crucial relations.

Imagine a hierarchy of languages: The lowest level tries to offer a pure phenomenological description of one's experience; the second level introduces a conceptual system of ordinary objects; the third moves on to the use of simple scientific concepts; the next, to the conceptual system of sophisticated scientific theories interwoven with metaphysical concepts and entities; and the last, to conceptual systems involving purely transcendental concepts belonging to some theology. I know this model is oversimplified. The language of mystics will involve several levels mixed together with additions that don't fit into the hierarchy. But the simplified hierarchy will enable me to make my point clearly.

Each level in the hierarchy provides a language that some mystic might employ in expressing his experience. Each level could be a legitimate language, no one of which is more true or more valid to the essential character of mysticism. No order of superiority is implied in the hierarchy. Different mystics might choose different levels as most appropriate. In trying to make a sharp separation of "nature" mysticism from "genuine" mysticism, Smart and Zaehner fail to see that each level in the hierarchy provides an appropriate and legitimate vehicle for the expression of mystical experience. To judge one level more correct than another manifests the author's unconscious commitment within some particular conceptual system.

To illustrate this hierarchy from the phenomenological to the transcendental, consider the following mystical claims:

(1) I feel a deep sense of inner quiet, calm, restfulness.

(2) My inner feeling of peace is impervious to outward events and changes involving the flux of ordinary objects.

(3) The unity I feel within my self is without motion or change.

(4) I sense my unity with all nature, timeless and spaceless.

(5) My soul touches God in a union blinded by the light of truth.

My point is that the mystic, seeking to express his experience, might employ any one or more of the five statements depending on the conceptual system and language making up the cultural-religious tradition to which he belongs, and that it is an arbitrary choice to divide mystical experience into types corresponding to one or more of the levels in the hierarchy. As philosophers seeking to understand mysticism we should look for the meaning of the mystic's claims within his language system. In this way we can best understand what he seeks to communicate.

Look at my sequence of statements. Present in each is a fundamental root experience referred to as quiet, peace, unity and union; an at-oneness-in-being. When the mystic tries to give his full expression to this experience, he makes use of the conceptual scheme and language of the tradition to which he belongs. Or the mystic as philosopher may have philosophic reasons for trying to employ one conceptual scheme rather than another. He may be a phenomenalist or realist or theist.

Notice how the statements move from subjective experience (quiet, calm, restfulness), to ordinary common sense objects (changes in objects), to metaphysical theories embracing all nature, to timelessness and spacelessness, and finally to transcendental theological doctrines about God (union blinded by the light of truth). I want to make clear that I do not suggest an order of inclusiveness or priority. Neither transcendence nor immanence, neither plurality nor unity is regarded as fundamental. Mystics have taken each of the possibilities as basic.

Against Smart and Zaehner, I think this analysis suggests that no sharp, definite line can be drawn separating genuine mysticism from nature mysticism. Each can occur depending upon the conceptual system ingredient in his language.

The second point I wish to make concerning Smart's paper deals with his claim that the meaning and validity of mystical experience depends upon the truth of some theology. This is so, Smart thinks, because the language used by the mystic involves in some degree the conceptual scheme of some theology. The mystic's language is more or less ramified with the concepts of some theology. These views raise a number of doubts in my mind to which it is very difficult to give a definite answer.

First, is it always the case that mysticism involves the conceptual scheme of some theology? If my earlier analysis of a hierarchy of conceptual levels is sound, then this would make possible a meaning and validity for mysticism without theological concepts. Such a mysticism could be expressed in any of the non-theological levels of my hierarchy. This is in fact what I think nature mysticism does. Or, if you will grant that certain pure forms of Buddhism do not contain a theology, then such Buddhist mysticism would escape from Smart's thesis.

Another old question is whether there can be mystical experience that is not expressed in any language and that does not propound any insights. Those mystics who assert the total ineffability of their experience would seem to present a mysticism wholly independent of the conceptual scheme of any theology. Since I do not know a decisive argument against such total ineffability, this would seem to refute Smart's position.

Smart's claim that the validity of mystical experience depends upon some theology seems to neglect the possibility that the mystical experience contains its own unique, direct justification. That mystics claim for their experience such self-contained justification is implicit in their use of it to criticize the theological tradition to which they belong. Time and again, mystics have claimed that their experience contains exactly this feature of direct authenticity, genuineness, certainty, and conviction. Such mystics never wait upon the examination of some theological arguments before accepting as true their mystical experience. Such behavior on the part of mystics makes clear, I think, that they do not depend upon theology to validate their experience.

I do not wish to deny that many mystics in their accounts make use of theological language; and whenever this is the case, some degree of validity is contributed by the assumed validity of that theology. But I should have supposed that the greater the amount of theological language involved in the mystic's account, the more doubtful we become of its purely mystical quality. What we encounter in cases where theological concepts abound is closer to a vision, an inspiration, or a relevation.

Another point that seems to count against Smart's position stems from those mystics who claim to pass beyond the limitations of any particular theology to a completely universal experience. Achievement of this experience beyond the differences of world theologies strongly suggests that their mysticism is independent of the validity of any particular theology. Ramakrishna would seem to be a case in point.[1]

[1] *Ramakrishna: Prophet of New India,* ed. and tr. Swami Nikhilananda, New York, 1942.

Whether or not mysticism rests upon some theological scheme for its validity depends upon a criterion of "theological scheme." If a mystic uses the term 'God,' does the validity of his mysticism thereby depend on some theology? I take "theology" and a "theological scheme" to involve a systematic account of the nature of God based on accessible evidence. If having mystical experience of God is, in itself, theology, then Smart has given us a mere tautology when he *links* the validity of mystical experience to some theology. If theology and mysticism are separate, Smart has not shown their necessary linkage. *Prima facie*, those mystics who experience God directly do not give us a theological system nor presuppose one.

A third point in Smart's paper about which I wish to raise some questions is his distinction between an auto-interpretation and a hetero-interpretation of mystical experience. An auto-interpretation is that offered by the mystic who had the experience; a hetero-interpretation is offered by someone else who did not have the mystical experience. Smart holds that both interpretations are affected by doctrinal schemes (which I assume to be the same as theological schemes). Smart leaves one with the impression that these interpretations are two similar but different perspectives on the same mystical experience, like looking at an object with different colored glasses. But I think the hetero-interpretation is derivative from and dependent upon an auto-interpretation because the mystical *experience* is a private affair. Someone else cannot have my experience. If I do not go on to offer an interpretation of my experience, then there is nothing available for someone else to interpret. The proper order in this situation is: first, the mystic's experience which is private to him; second, the mystic's auto-interpretation of his own experience; and third, the hetero-interpretation by someone else of the auto-interpretation of the mystic. There could be no hetero-interpretations unless the mystic first gave his own auto-interpretation. Auto-interpretation is primary and privileged. We don't have two interpretations of a common event but rather an interpretation (auto) of an event (experience) followed by an interpretation of the auto-interpretation. The mystic gives a report *of* his experience; the outsider gives a report *about* the mystic's report. There is an important difference in the logical type of these interpretations, for only the mystic can check his interpretations, only the mystic can check his interpretation against his experience. This privileged checking allows the mystic a pattern of justification (validity) that is not available to others. Smart's view that the validity is tied to some theological scheme arises partly from his improper account of auto- and hetero-interpretation.

My last query about Smart's paper is: Does he hold that the

same mystical experience can be given different valid interpretations, each of which is valid in some theology or doctrinal scheme? If this is his view, then how could a single mystical experience lead one to recast his doctrinal views? For he had already told us that the validity of the mystical experience depends on the interpreter's theology. Such recasting on Smart's view would seem to come from a re-examination of one's doctrinal schemes, after which a different interpretation is given to some mystical experience. Surely, some mystics would not be happy with this sequence of interpretation; otherwise, they would have no basis for radical and fundamental criticism of doctrinal systems.

Just to keep things lively, let me end with this barb. I suspect that the reason why Smart connects the validity of mystical experience to some theological scheme is his reluctance to free mysticism from theology as a prior and independent pivot for the religious life.

REJOINDERS

NINIAN SMART

I am grateful for the criticism. Let me first comment on the remarks of Mr. Pike. (Some of what I say is picked up from the points made in the discussion by those attending the symposium.)

1. Mr. Pike tries to impale me on the horns of a distinction between pictured-facts and non-pictured-facts. Let us look at his pictures.

(a) How do we know Picture B is of a man walking down a street (State Street, doubtless)? The artist *might* have intended the sign to show the name of the man. Or he could have mis-spelled something. Or the notice might be an *imperative*.

(b) The intentions of the artist come in because he is meaning to do something with the lines and what-not. He is thus importantly the authority (like a child puffing: he is the authority on whether he's a train or a mountaineer). This is not quite like the nirvāna case. Of course the saint is the authority on whether he is meaning to tread the Path that hopefully leads to nirvāna. But he is not the authority necessarily on whether what he attains is nirvāna. If we presuppose the truth of Buddhism it might be that the criteria for nirvāna-attainment are private (because they have to do with inner states), and so can only authoritatively be applied by the saint. But this does not make him an authority on the truth of the *doctrine* (e.g., that this state brings about a cessation of rebirth).

(c) But the last issue is about existence. Mr. Pike is right in pointing out that the phenomenology does not commit anyone to existence-claims. Still, *nirvāna* is a ramified concept. Where there is a gap between phenomenology and existence, there is also a gap between experience and interpretation.

2. I would not deny that, in the William James case cited by Mr. Pike, the sense of "another" is part of the phenomenology. Indeed it is characteristic of prophetism, *bhakti*, and their analogues to involve a "numinous" type of experience in which a gap, so to say, exists between the Other and the worshipper. My thesis only concerns those who are contemplatives in the sense indicated at the start of my paper.

3. Mr. Pike wants to refute my thesis by a single counter-example —the passage he quotes from Ruysbroeck. No one is sensibly going to abandon a good thesis because of a single apparent counter-example! But still, something ought to be said about it.

(a) I do not deny that theological notions may enter into the phenomenology of an experience. Theological notions in this way need not be extra-experiential. But this does not affect my central thesis. Consider feelings in the chest: they can be felt as pangs of indigestion. But a doctor could say: "These feelings arise from fluid in the lungs."

(b) The Ruysbroeck passage is not that impressive as a counter-example. Consider the second paragraph, which asserts that (1) the spirit feels identity with God ("one unit with God"); and (2) a distinction between the self and God is nevertheless felt because "there is an essential tending toward." Now it is characteristic of contemplative experience that the "subject-object" distinction does not apply—it is not like being here and seeing a flower over there, etc. On the other hand, in so far as there is an awareness on the part of the contemplative of where he has come from in arriving at the mystical experience, there is a sense of "tending toward" (whereas in God there is none such, it appears). The point can be paralleled very clearly in the Buddhist *jhānas* or stages of contemplation, where the sense of achievement in arriving at the higher contemplative state has to be set aside; i.e., one has to go on until there is no awareness of "tending toward," as there is no awareness of the environment, etc.

At the end of the first paragraph quoted from Ruysbroeck, we note significantly the use of the terms 'grace' and 'creature.' The "homeward-turning love" corresponds to the "tending toward": if the former involves an immediate awareness of the past, the latter involves an immediate anticipation of the cessation of the "union."

Hence I am not much impressed by the counter-example. It seems as much in my favor as against me.

I turn to Mr. Schmidt's remarks.

4. I liked the barb in the tail of his paper, and I agree with the main substance, as I understand it, of his comments. My thesis mainly concerns ramified descriptions; and I would not deny (and indeed explicitly affirmed) that we can have something less. But the correctness of an interpretation depends on two things: the nature of the experience (and here the mystic is privileged, as Mr. Schmidt rightly points out) and the truth of the presuppositions of the ramified description. Given this, I do not see that my contention about the connections between a ramified description and a theological scheme is wrong, even if it may partly rest on something improper, namely a lack of discussion about privacy and privilege.

5. Ramakrishna is not a good counter-example. He believed that modes of contemplation and devotion in different styles—Christian,

Hindu, Muslim, etc.—lead to the same goal. I was neither affirming nor denying this. Up to a point my thesis would seem to favor Ramakrishna's view, for if mystical experience is essentially the same everywhere, then, if one sort of mystical experience is valid, the others ought to be, too. But 'valid': what does this mean? It is only shorthand for saying that mystical experience gives the contemplative an apprehension of . . . Of what? Of God? If we say this, we are back with the question of the truth of a certain doctrinal scheme or set of doctrinal schemes (theistic ones), just as we are if we treat contemplative experience as a factor in bringing salvation or liberation. Besides, mystical experience is not the only sort of religious activity; nor is the mystical life the only form of the religious life. Much depends on how we evaluate mysticism in comparison with other modes of religious experience, etc.

6. Mr. Schmidt thinks that I hold or ought to hold that a mystic could have no basis for criticizing doctrinal systems. Not at all. If the contemplative thinks of himself as having "seen" God, he may come to criticize the theology in which he has been reared, and other theologies. Rightly so, for the character of the interior theophany may render silly many of the wooden and circumstantial things said about God. Likewise, having seen an historical person (e.g., Jesus) as revelatory of God one might revise one's prior beliefs. Mysticism is not the only basis for revisionary thinking, though it is one. But still the validity ("This is an experience of *God*") will depend on wider issues. It might also turn out that an evaluation of historical revelation ought to bring in mystical experience.

7. In brief, the fact that ramified descriptions of mystical experience occur in the literature should lead us away from a simple view of "validity"; and it should make us suspect that we need either many pigeon holes for the various supposed types, or just one. I plump for one. Pigeon holes are not to be multiplied beyond necessity.